Praise f

My friend Chip Ingram is one of my fav
point in applying God's truth to our lives.
Philippians three times so I know that we can never hit bottom in mining the joyful truths
in it. It has a mother lode of insight for your life.

RICK WARREN
Author, *The Purpose Driven Life*

When I read Chip's writings, it's like I'm having coffee with a wise, Christian mentor who
wants me to learn from his mistakes and experience. His rearview mirror will become your
windshield; and he will lovingly take you back to Jesus—the true source of joy.

DAVE STONE
Preacher and podcaster, *Pastor to Pastor with Dave Stone*

If you'd like a life defined by joy rather than anxiety, fear, or worry, you've found the right
guide. Chip Ingram masterfully unlocks God's path to change your life by changing your
thinking in this Bible-based study of joy. Read these words with an open heart, a prayerful
spirit, and watch God increase your joy. Practical and biblical, it's no exaggeration that the
truths in this book can change your life—or the life of someone you love.

JOHN S. DICKERSON
Nationally awarded journalist; author of *Jesus Skeptic*; Lead Pastor, Connection Pointe
Christian Church

In our postmodern culture, it seems that true joy is hard to come by. More people than ever
are wrestling with doubt and despair, and even committed Christians can find it difficult to
view their circumstances through a hopeful lens. In his latest book, Chip Ingram shows us
what genuine joy looks like and, even more importantly, how to cultivate it within our own
hearts and minds. No matter what you're facing, Chip's inspiring advice is sure to set you
on a path toward contagious, unshakable joy.

JIM DALY
President – Focus on the Family

Joy often seems so elusive, but it doesn't need to be. Joy is not dependent upon daily
circumstances. As Chip Ingram reflects upon various Scriptures, we learn joy is a choice,
a daily choice. Don't waste another day merely wishing for joy, learn to choose it and your
life will never be the same.

KYLE IDLEMAN
Senior pastor of Southeast Christian Church; bestselling author of *When Your Way Isn't Working*

In a turbulent world where it's easy to be tossed back and forth by our emotions and
ever-changing circumstances, Chip Ingram lays out a clear, biblical pathway to true joy in
I Choose Joy. Rather than being victims of our circumstances, Chip helps us reorient our
perspective—grounding it in God's character, His promises, and His eternal purposes. This
shift brings not only freedom but a deep, abiding joy that will make the world take notice.
Chip is a dear friend and a brilliant teacher, and his exposition of Philippians 1 is both practical and deeply needed in our time. This book will challenge and equip you to live with a
joy that is unshaken by life's difficulties and firmly anchored in Christ.

AARON PIERCE
President/CEO of Steiger International

Chip Ingram's life and ministry consistently challenge me to pursue Jesus more courageously—he is the real deal, a humble leader whose voice I deeply trust.

JENNIE ALLEN
Founder and visionary of IF:Gathering and Gather25; *NYT* bestselling author

I can think of no topic more important for the world than joy. And, knowing Chip as a pastor, author, and friend, I can confidently say there's no better person to unpack it than him. I've been immensely blessed by this book, and I know you will be too.

HENRY KAESTNER
Cofounder, BAND, Sovereign's Capital, FaithDrivenEntrepreneur.org, FaithDrivenInvestor.org, and GenerosityBayArea.org

My friend Chip Ingram has done it again. He has appropriately boxed us in and forced us to see the gospel benefit that is ours for the taking—joy. In *I Choose Joy*, Chip not only inspires us by communicating powerful principles from God's Word but offers authentic ways to make joy operational in every area of life. Chip is right: believers can fly above circumstances through a God-driven perspective. Read this book. Listen to God's Word. Live a transformed life.

MARK M. YARBROUGH
President, Dallas Theological Seminary

I loved this book! There are few people in the world who teach with such a clear, practical, and biblical way of bringing inspiration. I try to read everything Chip Ingram writes because I know the wisdom and takeaway value is always so good. *I Choose Joy* may be my favorite Chip Ingram book yet. You will learn how to put what he calls the "The Divine Equation" into your life. I closed the book and thought, *My circumstance may not change but my attitude can change and* that will make all the difference in the world.

JIM BURNS, PhD
Founder, HomeWord; author of *Doing Life with Your Adult Children: Keep Your Mouth Shut and the Welcome Mat Out*

My wife, Linda, and I have known, admired, and been kingdom coworkers with Chip for well over a decade. Once again, we find him a fount of spiritual insight, mental clarity, and now simply refreshment for our souls. Like many, the pandemic, social challenges, and life's uncertainty have lowered our joy. May you be lifted as we are to join Chip and choose joy.

PAT GELSINGER
CEO, Intel (retired); founder and chair, Transforming the Bay with Christ; Chair of the Board of Gloo

I CHOOSE

JOY

CHANGE YOUR PERSPECTIVE,
CHANGE YOUR LIFE.

CHIPINGRAM

Moody Publishers
CHICAGO

© 2025 by
Chip Ingram

Some names and details have been changed to protect the privacy of individuals.

Some content in this book has been adapted from the author's broadcast series "I Choose Joy," available on Living on the Edge's website: https://livingontheedge.org/broadcast-series/i-choose-joy/?media=daily.

Edited by: Cheryl Dunlop Molin
Cover design: Graham Terry and Thom Hoyman
Cover artwork: Thom Hoyman
Interior design: Kaylee Lockenour Dunn

ISBN: 978-0-8024-3726-6

Originally delivered by fleets of horse-drawn wagons, the affordable paperbacks from D. L. Moody's publishing house resourced the church and served everyday people. Now, after more than 125 years of publishing and ministry, Moody Publishers' mission remains the same—even if our delivery systems have changed a bit. For more information on other books (and resources) created from a biblical perspective, go to www.moodypublishers.com or write to:

Moody Publishers
820 N. LaSalle Boulevard
Chicago, IL 60610

1 3 5 7 9 10 8 6 4 2

Printed in the United States of America

To the fabulous team at Living on the Edge,
who have been a source of incredible joy in my life and ministry.

Contents

Introduction

Who is the most joyful person you know? Stop—don't keep on reading. I want you to really think about the most joyful person you know. How do you feel when you're around them? What is it that they have and how would you describe it?

I light up when I think of the most joyful people I know. They're fun to be around, the atmosphere changes when they walk into a room. I can feel down and struggling and after ten minutes with one of them, something shifts inside of me. Their joy is contagious, encouraging. It makes me want to be around them more.

But something has happened in the last several years. The joy quotient for most people, even followers of Jesus, has taken a dive. Without rehashing all the negative long-term outcomes of Covid, let's be honest, it was like a dark cloud that hovered over the whole earth, and some of us continue to be affected by it to this day.

It's not just about the tragedy of lost loved ones, lost jobs, economic implosion, social isolation, or kids who missed school and now live with anxiety daily; our hangover started with the pandemic and then multiplied as the division in our country escalated. Churches and families were split apart over vaccines and masks and political issues. Social media and cable news outlets stoked the fires. The national atmosphere shifted to such a degree that it seems there's no noninflammatory events in the world anymore, but someone to blame for whatever happens, and it's "the other group's fault."

My own joy level took a dramatic dip over the last few years. I had two very serious back surgeries with the second one occurring in the middle of Covid. The rehabs were long, and the restrictions were great. I took long, slow walks with baby steps as I sought to recover. Toward the end of that recovery, my wife, Theresa, said in a very kind but penetrating way, "Do you realize how negative you've become?" I shot back a quick defensive response, explaining all the difficult circumstances that I'd been through. But her words stung and stuck deep in my heart.

The truth is, I was complaining inside, even when I wasn't saying anything negative on the outside. My internal self-talk was critical of myself and just about everything and everyone else. Every circumstance, relationship, and even ministry progress was viewed with an unconscious lens of seeing what was missing, what was half full, what didn't measure up, and in my weakest moments, whose fault it was.

> **The truth is, I was complaining inside, even when I wasn't saying anything negative on the outside.**

During this time God led me to teach Philippians 1 to a group at the Billy Graham Conference Center in Asheville, North Carolina. I knew the material, but I had no idea what the material was going to do to me.

It's one thing to talk about joy, teach about joy, know how joy is supposed to work; but it's quite another to really experience joy authentically when times are tough and circumstances aren't going your way.

As I studied the text, I was reminded of Nehemiah's words that "the joy of the LORD is your strength" (Neh. 8:10). My research led me to a classic C. S. Lewis quote where he reminds us that "Joy is the serious business of Heaven."[1] Somehow along the way, I had given myself permission to have a so-so attitude and explain to myself, with all the negativity in the world, all the challenges I'd been through, that it's "okay" to not be as upbeat, pleasant, and joyful as I used to be.

Don't get me wrong, I could still explain to people that joy has to do with God's Spirit working in us, and it is a by-product of an intimate relationship with Him regardless of the circumstances. I could clearly articulate that joy is different from happiness, which is rooted in the happenings of our life. When circumstances are good, we're happy; when circumstances are bad, we're not.

Yes, I've heard people say it's not worth splitting hairs over the difference between happiness and joy, but there certainly is a difference; one is primarily based on our emotions and circumstances, and the other is a by-product of the Spirit of God working within us. The first is primarily external, while the second is primarily internal as the Spirit of God produces the fruit of Christlikeness in and through us, regardless of our external circumstances or challenges.

It was hard for me to face as I began to recognize that in small ways, and sometimes big ways, I was far more negative than I used to be. I thought Covid and all the changes in our culture had affected other people, but somehow, I assumed it hadn't affected me . . . or at least not that much. However, nothing could be further from the truth.

Little by little, I came to the conclusion that I needed to make some changes. Joy, just like love, peace, and kindness, are charistics of the fruit of the Spirit that need to be a vibrant part of my life. So, I did what I normally do when I see that I need to change; I chose two or three verses that talk about joy, wrote them on a 3x5 card, and memorized the verses, repeating them throughout the day. It helped. In fact, it helped quite a bit, but not as much as I thought.

FAILURE TO COMMUNICATE

About this time, I had a unique opportunity to get some coaching on my communication skills. A friend had a relationship with the number one communication coaching organization in America. They are the "go-to" resource to help top Silicon Valley CEOs make their very best presentations, and he offered a day alone with their president for free to up my game.

We chatted on the phone about what the goals of our time would be, and he asked me to send a few videos of my teaching. His father had started the company years earlier. He was a super nice guy, so we lined up a time to meet.

After he arrived, we talked casually, and then he had me speak into the camera in our video recording studio. It was very impromptu, and then we sat and talked about where I could improve.

After he watched my teaching videos the president provided feedback. "We think you're a good communicator. You know your material well; you really connect with people. And, unless you're faking it, we think you're very authentic. But there was something missing that I couldn't put my finger on. So I asked my father after watching the videos, 'What do you think? Where do you think we could help this guy get better?' It was then that he said the one thing that I realized was the very thing I couldn't put my finger on."

My curiosity was piqued. He then asked me to come and watch

the two-minute video he recorded of me. Just minutes earlier, he threw out a topic with the camera running and said, "Give me two or three minutes about how God feels about all the people in the world." It was totally off the cuff, with no preparation. I spontaneously gave my best two minutes of how our great God cares for and loves everyone. He motioned me to come over to watch the short video we had just made.

When we stood over the lens together, he asked me, "What do you see?"

I said, "I see a guy who's pretty passionate about telling the world that God really does care and loves them."

Then he said something that shocked me, "I see that too, but notice how intense you look, how serious the message is. Notice you don't smile at all." Then he turned off the sound and asked me, "Does this person speaking look like they're very joyful and that they're communicating about God's great love?"

> **If Theresa's comment months earlier had stung, this was like a sword through my heart.**

If Theresa's comment months earlier had stung, this was like a sword through my heart. "I don't know you very well," he said, "and you obviously have a significant communication gift, but if there's one thing I could say that would help you communicate better, it would be 'lighten up.' Smile more when you talk. Let people know by your smile and tone the same message that you're saying with your words." Then he looked at me and said, "You're really an intense guy!"

CHOOSING JOY

In the providence of God, I was to teach Philippians 1 with the title "I Choose Joy" to a group of Christians who had weathered the pain of divisions, family struggles, cancer, wayward children, depression, and a culture that seemed to become more and more anti-Christian overnight. If there was ever a time to help people understand and experience God's joy in the midst of adversity, this was it. I could almost hear Mr. Phelps of *Mission Impossible* speaking to me from the recorder that will self-destruct in thirty seconds, saying, "Your mission, should you choose to accept it, is to help this group grasp that joy isn't something that comes and goes depending on our circumstances or relationships—but in fact, it is a *choice* that we make each and every day."

So, I began by giving them the context of this passage. The apostle Paul was in prison writing this letter. He was awaiting execution, or acquittal—he had no idea which it would be. He had been abandoned by close friends, betrayed by fellow Christians who used his imprisonment to criticize him and promote themselves, and was enduring the conditions of a first-century prison.

In this short chapter, Paul gives us his secret of joy in any and every circumstance. He helps us understand that it's a matter of focus, a matter of purpose, a matter of hope, and a matter of expectations.

I don't know what's going on in your life, but I do know the "Joy Quotient" among fellow followers of Jesus has taken a big hit. My prayer for you is that our time together in this book will bring about a renaissance not just in your emotions, but in your focus, in your attitude, and in your relationships with the Lord and others.

Joy isn't just possible, it's commanded: "Rejoice in the Lord always; again I will say, rejoice! Let your gentle spirit be known to all men" (Phil. 4:4–5).

When I began teaching this series, I had a high round table off to my left with a huge pitcher of water on top of it. I had the pitcher filled exactly to the middle of its capacity. Before opening the text, I said in a lighthearted manner, "How many people think this pitcher is half full?" Lots of hands went up. Then I said, "How many of you think this pitcher is half empty?" And a lot of hands went up. "Guess what?" I said smiling. "You're both right!"

Certain things happen in life that we have no control over. Many of those things are painful and disappointing. How we look at them will make all the difference in the world. How we process them will either make or break us, often impacting deeply those around us.

May God in His grace allow you and me to learn from our brother the apostle Paul how to "choose joy" regardless of what's happening around us or to us.

My prayer is that when someone who knows you is asked, "Who is the most joyful person that you know?" their answer would be you.

CHAPTER 1:

The Power of Focus

Bobby was a friend and a neighbor. He was gregarious, a success-ful businessman, a mover and shaker who was always active, either working or headed off on a ski trip to Vail or spending time on his boat. At first, we talked casually whenever we saw each other out in the yard, but over time, the conversations went deeper and covered a lot of topics. We got to know each other well.

Eventually, I learned a little about Bobby's faith. He had known God, gone to church regularly, and knew all the Christian lingo. He said he loved Jesus and would have even described himself as being born again. However, he had backed away from it all. He just wasn't into it anymore. He was what we might call a cultural Christian—a nominal believer who knew the truth, but was no longer fully engaged with living it out.

Bobby was a cabinet maker. His warehouse was full of top-quality cabinets ready to be installed in luxury homes for contracts worth hundreds of thousands of dollars. One Sunday morning as I was pulling out of my driveway to go to church, Bobby's wife came out and waved me down.

"Please pray for us," she said. "Bobby's warehouse burned down. We think it was arson. We've lost everything and don't have insurance to cover it."

Later when I saw Bobby out in the yard, he looked like someone had died. Over the next few months, I could look across the street and see Bobby sitting in a chair, staring out his bay window, almost as if he were in some kind of catatonic state. Sometimes he took long walks around the block. He was depressed for a long time. He lived like someone who thought his life was over.

> **Within minutes, the whole warehouse was on fire, and once again, Bobby lost everything in it.**

We had a lot of conversations during that time, and somewhere along the way, he decided to get closer to God through this experience.

Some entrepreneurs just know how to make money. I've heard of multimillionaires who have gone bankrupt and then made all their money back like nothing had happened. Bobby had that ability. He was resilient. About four years after his loss, he had built his business up again. He had another warehouse, filled it with materials and finished cabinets, and was once again making a lot of money. This time he had a little insurance too—not to cover everything, but at least enough to provide some protection against another loss.

Bobby was easy to get along with and had several master craftsmen who loved working for him. One of them went into the warehouse to help clean up one day, and as he was working on a blowtorch, it sparked some sawdust that quickly went up in flames. Within minutes, the whole warehouse was on fire, and once again, Bobby lost everything in it. Having a little insurance helped avoid a total loss, but the fire essentially ruined his business a second time.

I found out the way I did the first time—when his wife came out as I was pulling out of the driveway. I told her I would pray for them and braced myself to see Bobby go through another very difficult season.

But the next time I saw Bobby, I could tell he wasn't taking it as hard as the last time. I asked him how he was doing.

"When I heard the news," he told me, "everything in me just wanted to break down. But I told my wife, 'Stay right here. I'm going to walk around the block.' As I started to walk, I started praying: 'Naked I came into the world, and naked I will return. The Lord gives, and the Lord takes away. Blessed be the name of the Lord.'"[2]

Then he started thanking God, "'Lord, thank You that I have a wife who is loyal and cares for me. Thank You for my son and my grandson. Thank You for all the loving people You've put in my life.' I choose to give thanks and focus on what I do have, not what I lost."

Within forty-eight hours, Bobby had called around to his business competitors and found work for all of his craftsmen. It was a total contrast to his experience after the first fire. He didn't get depressed. His workers didn't have long to be discouraged or jobless. I asked him why it was different this time.

"When this happened, I knew I had been through it before and come out of it okay," he said. "Before, my whole life was about things. Nothing that can be lost so easily can satisfy. I know what matters now."

That doesn't mean it was easy. Bobby had lost a lot of money and didn't have any cabinets to fulfill his contracts. He knew he was going to go through another difficult season. It would take time to rebuild again. "But I've got a lot," he told me as we stood in his yard watching his grandson play. "I've got a great family, and I've reconnected with God. Yes, I've got a lot."

IS THE GLASS HALF FULL OR HALF EMPTY?

It's easy to choose joy when things are going well. But what about when they aren't?

We all go through trials and difficult seasons. Sometimes circumstances are very painful and challenging. Yet Scripture tells us even in those difficult circumstances to choose joy. And Jesus promised we could have it—not only when it's easy but even in the most challenging times of our lives.

> The difference is not the glass or the water in it. It's how we see it

How is that possible? Choosing joy in the midst of difficulties goes against all our instincts. When things go wrong, it's easy to look inward and fall into self-pity. Before long, our life is spiraling downward.

It doesn't have to be that way. As we look at Paul's words in the first chapter of his letter to the Philippians, we will see that joy really is a choice and that God will give us everything we need, no matter how difficult and devastating our circumstances might be. In Paul's teaching and his example, we will learn the power of focus.

We already know the power of focus—in principle. It shapes our perspective. We even use a very common idiomatic expression for it: "Is the glass half full or half empty?" Depending on your perspective, you'd either notice that there's water in the glass or that the water doesn't fill the glass. One focuses on the positive—what's there. The other focuses on the negative—what isn't there. And even if one person sees it one way and another sees it the other way, they are both right, aren't they? The difference is not the glass or the water in it. It's how we see it. We evaluate it according to the perspective we bring to it. Before I started teaching this series, I put the pitcher of water center stage to make this very point.

Some people spend their entire lives focused on what they don't have, what's wrong, what they wish was better, what God hasn't provided, and what they think they need for the joy and happiness they don't already have. And you'd be surprised—some people do that even when other people would envy them for all the wonderful gifts and blessings they have. Even when our lives are filled with good things, many of us have a tendency to focus on whatever is still lacking or needs to be fixed.

Other people have learned to focus on what they do have. They realize that everyone's life has some degree of emptiness. Everyone struggles at work and home. Everyone has problematic relationships and, sooner or later, health issues. We all suffer sometimes. But instead of letting those challenges define them, they see the blessings they've already been given. And because that's their focus, they are empowered to remember God's goodness and sovereignty even in life's most challenging situations.

> **Perspective, or focus, is one of the keys to joy.**

Perspective, or focus, is one of the keys to joy. And as we'll see, it's something we choose.

Bobby experienced both of these perspectives. After his first fire, his focus was inward. He was acutely aware of everything he'd lost and could hardly focus on what he still had—and what was much more valuable than what he had lost.

After the second fire, his focus was upward and then outward. The situation hadn't changed; both times, his business was devastated by fire, and he lost almost everything. But his perspective had changed dramatically. He learned how to choose his focus.

How can we develop the kind of perspective that transcends our circumstances? That's the key question everyone has to answer—

not just once but daily, even moment to moment. We don't have to wonder if we'll experience tough circumstances. We will. Everyone does. The issue is how we deal with them.

THE DIVINE EQUATION

If you've ever thought your experience of joy is random or that it depends on the circumstances you go through, I've got news for you: There's nothing random about it. We may not be able to choose all our circumstances, but we can choose how we see them. And that choice determines whether or not we live in joy.

If we were to put that principle in the form of an equation, it would look something like this:

> **THE DIVINE EQUATION: C + P = E**
> **Circumstance + Perspective = Experience**
>
> Living above my circumstances occurs when my **perspective** interprets my circumstances rather than my **circumstances** determining my perspective.

You might want to write this formula on an index card and put it where you will see it often. Reminding yourself that there's a different way to see things is one way to shift your perspective.

Maybe you're wondering why an equation like this—something that looks very mathematical and formulaic—is so important. The Christian life is not a formula, of course, but God gives us some guiding principles that have a profound influence on the trajectory of our lives. This is one of them. It's rock-solid truth, and it's demonstrated for us clearly in Scripture as a model for training our minds and hearts to see the truth and live it out.

This is critical to a life of joy. Joy comes from learning to live above your circumstances. You will either let your circumstances determine your perspective or let your perspective determine your circumstances. Those are your only two options. You can probably guess which one leads to greater joy.

Crises, tragedies, and even normal hardships are a part of life in this fallen world. For many people, they represent major turning points. Some people are broken by them and grow bitter, sink into their regrets, and blame God and others for what they have been through. Others are drawn closer to God through them and come out with greater faith and a clear perspective on what's important and what isn't.

What's the difference? Why are some people filled with despair and bitterness while others are filled with joy—even when they've gone through similar situations? The answer is in that equation. Your circumstances don't determine your experience. Your circumstances *plus your perspective* determines your experience. The fundamental issue is how we can develop the kind of perspective that transcends our circumstances.

It isn't that hard to see how dramatically our responses to hardships can change the course of our lives. Some people have unconsciously made an assumption about life with God—that if you love God and are a good person trying to serve Him, then bad things won't happen to you and your loved ones. Your family members will be spared from cancer and drunk drivers, your kids will become faithful believers, and life will generally go well because God is taking care of you.

That assumption gets shattered sometimes, and people who aren't grounded in a biblical perspective don't know how to deal with the aftermath. They feel as if God has let them down. As you can imagine, that undermines faith and leaves little room for joy.

This is why perspective is so important.

Think about how this might have played out in your life. When you look at life through the lens of your circumstances, what happens? You're happy when circumstances are good, and sad or angry when they aren't, right? But if you look at your circumstances through the lens of God's goodness—His power and promises—that's a higher perspective. You can experience joy because you know a good God is going to take even the worst and most difficult things in life and use them for your good.

Living above our circumstances occurs when our perspective interprets our circumstances rather than our circumstances determining our perspective.

That's the answer to the question we asked above. How can we transcend our circumstances? The answer is perspective: C + P = E.

LESSONS FROM THE LIFE OF PAUL

In Philippians 1, Paul gives us four keys and four questions that will determine whether we live with the joy God has promised to give us. We'll look at the first key and first question in this chapter and the next.

KEY #1: FOCUS
QUESTION #1: WHERE IS MY FOCUS?

What is your most challenging, difficult, painful circumstance or relationship right now? What weighs you down or keeps you up at night? If you could pick one thing for God to fix or take away, what would it be?

Now with that in mind, let's look at Philippians 1. This chapter is especially powerful when we know the context. Paul is likely writing to the Philippian believers from captivity in Rome. He has already been beaten on numerous occasions, spent a night floating at sea, been stoned and left for dead once, and has been opposed in many ways and on many fronts throughout his ministry. God had called him to take the message of the gospel to the gentile world, and he has been single-mindedly focused on it ever since he received that calling. But it hasn't been easy, and his opponents in Jerusalem stirred up a crowd and had him arrested. He spent two years in legal limbo in Judea before being shipped to Rome, where he has continued to await his trial. And while he waits, he writes this letter.

From a purely human perspective, Paul had a right to be discouraged.

Paul didn't know how influential this letter and the others he wrote while in Rome would be. All he knew was that God had sent him on this mission to reach people with the gospel, and he had eagerly followed his calling. Yet he had been opposed every step of the way, sometimes violently. He was under house arrest (Acts 28:16, 30), which meant he could receive visitors and have some limited privileges in a rented home or apartment (at his expense). But he was still watched by a Roman guard constantly, probably chained at night, and unable to establish new churches or build up the ones he had already started—at least in person.

From a purely human perspective, Paul had a right to be discouraged. And if he looked at his life through the lens of his circumstances, he would have been. It seemed as if his entire ministry was compromised and at a standstill. This could have been a glass-half-empty moment for him.

But that's not the perspective he presented to the Philippian believers. His letter to them is full of joy. In fact, probably very surprisingly to his readers, it's *overflowing* with joy.

Paul had a strong heart connection with this church. He and they had a lot of affection for each other, as the church was blessed and grew through some significant challenges. The believers in Philippi had heard that Paul was confined in Rome and, since prisoners under house arrest were responsible for paying their own lodging and other living expenses, they knew he needed support. So, they sent him a financial gift through one of their members, Epaphroditus, and this letter is Paul's response to them.

In this letter, Paul took advantage of the opportunity not only to thank them but also to address some of the issues they were facing, which Epaphroditus would have talked about with him in some detail. And one of those issues was their concern for Paul and all he was going through.

Even from the start, this letter is full of affection. After a greeting from himself and Timothy, who was apparently with Paul at this time, he tells them how he feels about them:

> I thank my God in all my remembrance of you, always offering prayer with joy in my every prayer for you all, in view of your participation in the gospel from the first day until now. For I am confident of this very thing, that He who began a good work in you will perfect it until the day of Christ Jesus. (Phil. 1:3–6)

Notice the key words in this passage that tell us something about Paul's perspective, particularly "thank," "remembrance," "prayer with joy," and "confident." Does he seem worried about his situation and how it might turn out? Not at all. As he has prayed for all the believers in this church, he has maintained a very positive perspective, full of joy and gratitude.

Paul's Upward Focus

Remember where Paul is. He is confined in Rome, under constant guard and at least figuratively if not literally in chains, awaiting a trial that could result either in his freedom or his death. He has spent years going from place to place to preach and teach the message of Jesus to Jews and gentiles alike, establishing many churches and training many disciples. But at this moment, he is unable to do any of that, and as far as he knows, he may never be able to travel and teach again.

You might recall what happened to Paul on his first visit to Philippi (Acts 16:11–40). After preaching and teaching for many days, Paul and Silas found themselves at the center of a controversy and were thrown in a jail cell after being brutally beaten with thick, bone-breaking rods. As they sat in the dark, chained and shackled in probably painful positions, they prayed and sang hymns. God responded miraculously with an earthquake that broke their chains and opened locked doors, and the Philippian jailer and his family received Jesus as their Savior. Paul knew what it was like to worship in a crisis and see God move powerfully to bring good out of it.

That experience may have happened a decade or more before Paul wrote this letter, but many believers in Philippi would remember it well. They might need to be comforted in his current crisis, but apparently he did not. Even though he was going through alarming circumstances, he became the comforter and encourager, and they would have been heartened by his assurances that he prayed for them "with joy."

They were also encouraged by the reason Paul remembered them with joy when he prayed. As he tells them, it was "in view of [their] participation in the gospel" from the beginning of his ministry among them. In other words, "we were in this together, and we still are." Paul was filled with gratitude because they and he had seen God work in that city. He was thankful for his lasting relationship with these fellow believers.

Paul is not only joyful and grateful in this letter but also optimistic. His focus in this passage is not on himself but on God and the believers in this young church. He is "confident" that God is in control—that He will continue working in them as He has in the past.

Paul could have been full of concerns about himself. No one would blame him. He could have talked about his difficult living conditions, chains that kept him close to his guard, rats in the building, lack of funds to pay for his food, frustrations about being silenced by an ungodly government, or any number of other complaints. He could have focused on his innocence and how unfair his whole situation was. But blaming God or others and complaining about circumstances reflects an inward focus. Paul refused to go there. He knew God was still on His throne no matter how challenging his situation looked.

> Paul's words focus not on circumstances, but on the heartfelt connection he has with this church.

That's an upward focus, not an inward one, and it's powerful. It reflects an attitude of trust in God and gratitude for what He has done, is doing, and will continue to do in the future. Someone who focuses upward has no need to live in regret, cast blame, or feel despair. *When we know God is taking care of us and is sovereign over all our circumstances, we can live with gratitude and joy.*

As you consider the truth in the last paragraph, it is deeply encouraging, but very challenging. I mentioned in the introduction that

I've had lots of struggles putting this into practice. Closing out this section on Paul's upward focus, I want to share one thing that has helped me the most. Singing doesn't come naturally to me, but as I was on my personal *restore my joy* journey, one of the things that has helped me the most is to spend time singing to the Lord. My son is a worship leader, and I often select songs he's written because they're close to my heart. I often sing them in my office as I start my day. I don't know how to explain it, because yes, praying is important, and yes, I'm in God's Word, but there is something powerful about lifting our voices to Jesus and hearing music that floods over our souls, that draws us near in a way that mere intellectual truth or even praying doesn't. Let me encourage you to give it a try to develop your upward focus.

Paul's Outward Focus

Paul reflected very little on his own situation. He was more concerned for these believers and how they were doing in their circumstances in Philippi. Though they were not nearly as challenging to work with as some of the other churches Paul founded, they had their issues, both in the opposition they faced in Philippi and in their relationships within their church. Still, Paul was confident that God was going to keep working in them until Jesus' return.

Then Paul explained why:

> For it is only right for me to feel this way about you all, because I have you in my heart, since both in my imprisonment and in the defense and confirmation of the gospel, you all are partakers of grace with me. For God is my witness, how I long for you all with the affection of Christ Jesus. (Phil. 1:7–8)

Notice the key words Paul uses to express his perspective, especially those that express his emotions: "feel," "heart," "partakers . . .

with me," "long," and "affection." He is not reluctant to tell them how he feels about them or to remind them of the connection they have with him and with each other. This is a very relational letter—that makes sense, because the gospel and God's kingdom are relational at their core—so Paul's words focus not on circumstances, but on the heartfelt connection he has with this church. He is genuinely concerned about their welfare.

Imagine hearing about a dear friend who is going through an incredibly difficult time—severe financial hardship and a recent cancer diagnosis—and sending them an email to ask how they are doing and if there is anything you can do help. How would you feel if this was the response that came back: "Every time I think of you, I pray for you! I remember our times together, and I long for more of them. I just have so much affection for you!"

> Paul was not a victim of circumstances, and neither are we.

It would be a little shocking, wouldn't it? You would expect your friend to start by talking about his or her struggles, not to focus on you and express gratitude for your relationship.

Notice that Paul doesn't just talk about his own affection. He longs for them *with the affection of Christ.* Jesus has put His own affection for these people within Paul's heart. This is an expression of divine love.

I memorized this passage many years ago and remember praying, "Lord, I don't know if I could ever say that to anyone, but I would love to able to do so—to someday, somehow love, long for, and care for someone in the same way Jesus cares for me." There is nothing self-centered or self-absorbed in that kind of love. It's a completely outward focus. Paul was so filled up with love for other people that he seemed almost unaware of his circumstances.

That kind of love leads naturally into prayer. Not only does Paul tell them he has been praying for them (vv. 3–4); but he also tells them what he has been praying.

> And this I pray, that your love may abound still more and more in real knowledge and all discernment, so that you may approve the things that are excellent, in order to be sincere and blameless until the day of Christ; having been filled with the fruit of righteousness which comes through Jesus Christ, to the glory and praise of God. (Phil. 1:9–11)

Paul essentially tells them, "My focus isn't on myself and my imprisonment. It's on God first and also on you, and I want you to know what I'm praying for you. I'm asking God that your love and relationships would grow deeper and deeper in the knowledge of God."

This "knowledge" (*epignosis*) is a very powerful word. It's not just head knowledge; it's real and experiential. Paul wants them to have a profound, ongoing experience with God that leads to deep discernment and understanding. In other words, he is asking that they would get so close to God in the midst of this corrupt Roman culture and all the opposition it brings against believers—him in Rome and the members of this church in the Roman colony of Philippi—that they would "approve the things that are excellent." His prayer is that when the world comes against them, they would know from experiencing and interacting with God Himself what is right, wrong, good, true, false, and every other insight that helps them know how to live their lives.

Why? After praying that the Philippians' love would keep growing and deepening, Paul uses a very important but easily unnoticed phrase: "so that." He wants them to abound in knowledge of God "so that" they will be "sincere and blameless until the day of Christ; having been filled with the fruit of righteousness which comes through Jesus Christ, to the glory and praise of God."

Out of all the things Paul could have focused on, that's what he chose. And focus really is a choice. We must learn to see it as one. Paul was not a victim of circumstances, and neither are we. We are rooted in God, connected in love, and growing in truth and righteousness for His glory and praise. I confess, this is a constant battle for me. When negative circumstances come my way, I catch my thoughts "going negative," feeling like a victim, or blaming someone for my misfortune; I say out loud C + P = E (Circumstance + Perspective = Experience) and refocus upward and outward.

A FOCUS THAT LEADS TO JOY

> Maintaining that upward and outward focus isn't always easy to do, but it is possible with practice over time.

I don't know what you're going through right now. Whatever it is may be extremely difficult. But whether you are enjoying good times or struggling through the greatest challenges of your life, God's Word always points us to a higher reality than surviving our circumstances and navigating the situations we face. We can choose to lift our eyes, embrace the higher vision, and live in gratitude and joy.

That is not a onetime choice. It's daily, even minute by minute. You can choose to look at God, other people, and life itself through the lens of your circumstances, but when circumstances are not good, that focus will only lead to frustration, bitterness, and despair.

Or, you can learn from Paul and look up and out. His circumstances were as bad as anyone's. He could have faced execution in the very near future. He had no way of knowing for sure. While he waited, he endured the frustration of captivity and a very long break in his traveling, preaching and teaching, and church planting ministry. In the midst of those challenges, he kept his upward and outward focus, trusting God and building up the people around him.

Maintaining that upward and outward focus isn't always easy to do, but it is possible with practice over time. Paul expressed this perspective from the very beginning of this letter to the Philippians, and if we look closely enough, we can see how he has developed it. As the letter continues, Paul by example demonstrated again and again how we can have that focus, too, and live all of life with an attitude of *joy* even in the midst of our deepest challenge.

DISCUSSION/APPLICATION QUESTIONS

1. What's the most challenging circumstance you're currently facing?

2. Where is your current focus: inward, upward, or outward?

3. What factors and/or people tend to reinforce a negative or inward "victim mentality" in your life?

4. From what you learned in this chapter, what specific steps could you take toward changing your focus and your perspective?

Assignment: Share with one trusted person your specific application to question 4 and ask them to pray for you.

CHAPTER 2:

How to Develop Your Focus

Good habits are hard to develop and bad habits are hard to break. This is especially true when it comes to mindsets. My negative mindset that gradually developed after back surgeries, setbacks, and the pandemic unconsciously became a habit. I wasn't trying to be joyless and negative or complaining; but little by little it was leaking out of my words, my attitude, and apparently even my behavior.

I had a blind spot and was not even aware of it until my wife and a consultant were used by God to help me see it. But seeing it and doing something about it are two very different things.

I tried really hard for a couple weeks to be more positive, upbeat. I said to myself, "I'm a positive person, God loves me, I have so much going for me, I'm just going to be more positive and joyful." Unfortunately, habits don't die easily, and ones you didn't even know you had die even more slowly.

After a few weeks, I recognized that my "try hard to do better" behavior modification wasn't working. As I continued to study Paul's example in Philippians 1, I was reminded of what he taught in Romans 12:2, "Do not be conformed to this world, but be transformed by *the renewing* of your *mind*, so that you may prove what the will of God is, that which is good and acceptable and perfect" (italics added).

> I realized I needed to change my focus and my outlook, and that meant I needed to change my thinking.

I realized I needed to change my focus and my outlook, and that meant I needed to change my thinking. In this chapter we will observe how the apostle Paul models this for us, and talk about some very practical ways to break the thought patterns and habits that warp our perspective and steal our joy.

SHIFTING YOUR FOCUS UPWARD

Paul was exceptional in a lot of ways. No one else in the early church did more to reach gentiles with the message of the gospel, and no one else (aside from Jesus) did so much to shape our understanding of salvation. Because of his monumental place in the New Testament, we tend to see Paul as a super-apostle—a great example, but an example we can never hope to live up to.

But that isn't how Paul saw himself, and it isn't an accurate picture of his spiritual life or ours. Paul struggled with many of the same things we do. In fact, he was saved out of a background far worse than most believers can imagine. He did not naturally choose joy. He had to learn it—just like we do.

We therefore need to resist the temptation to read Paul's words in Philippians and think, *Well, that's Paul. Glad he can look at things that way. I'm not nearly there yet.* No matter how difficult we think this is, it's doable. God even empowers us to do it. Paul's example really is meant for each and every one of us.

How do we develop an upward focus like Paul had? I believe there are three keys to this dramatic shift in perspective, and we can see them right there in Philippians 1:3–6, a passage we looked at in the last chapter.

A Choice

It begins with a choice, and that choice is gratitude. We choose to remember significant relationships and thank God for them.

Our ministry has a weekly prayer time that is led by different people each week. One week, a young staff member began by handing out index cards. He told us we would need two or three, so I took several, thinking that would be more than enough. Then he explained what we were to do with them. He said he would give us twenty minutes to write down everything we were thankful for, starting with as many people as we could remember in that time. "Just don't stop writing," he said.

The first few were easy—my wife, my children, other family members. I wrote their names one by one. By then I was on a roll. I wrote down the people in my church, the people I get to work with, the friends and neighbors I get to live with in this crazy world, people who have walked with me through hard times, just doing life together. I thanked God for forgiveness and salvation, His Spirit living in me, the calling He had given me, all the churches I've been a part of. People and experiences kept coming to mind, some I hadn't thought about in years; and I kept writing as fast as I could.

Writing front and back in very small print, I filled up five cards easily. And I could have kept going.

Most of us have the tendency to focus on whatever is wrong and needs to be fixed or whatever has been disappointing and still feels like a loss.

It took me a while to figure out why I had such a great day until I made the connection. Someone had made me sit for twenty minutes and do nothing but think of what I was thankful for. God's love and goodness flooded over me as I realized how kind and generous He has been to me. He has filled my life with wonderful, supportive people, and given me rewarding opportunities to serve Him and enjoy His good gifts. I was still aware of all the ups and downs I'd experienced—and some of the downs were extremely painful and difficult—but I felt so grateful for all God has done. I had a great attitude all day long.

Most of us have the tendency to focus on whatever is wrong and needs to be fixed, or whatever has been disappointing and still feels like a loss. Even when the glass is almost full, we tend to focus on what's missing because we want more. That's not necessarily wrong—we're designed to keep improving and advancing—but it can lead to a very distorted perspective.

I've seen this play out again and again in many lives. It's why people who seem to have everything can be miserable. I know people who are envied for their family and friends, all the accomplishments they've achieved, and all the material blessings they've been given, and they still aren't happy because they keep striving for bigger, better, and more. If they stopped and thought about all the goodness God has poured into their lives, they would be overwhelmed with gratitude.

That's the first step in living with an upward focus that leads to joy. Be thankful, especially for your relationship with God and with the people He has put in your life.

An Action

In his gratitude for the Philippian believers, Paul willfully chose to remember them "with joy" in "every prayer" for them (v. 4). In order to develop an upward focus, we need to pray. However, whenever we can, we need to pray *with joy*.

That means praying with joy even when you don't feel like it. Prayer can involve the warm-and-fuzzy feelings we love to have, but very often those feelings aren't there. That doesn't mean we don't have a connection with God and can't pray with

———

God doesn't expect you to manufacture feelings or go through the motions.

———

joy. Sometimes the most rewarding prayer experiences are those we choose to have even when we aren't in the mood.

I've had a lot of issues with my back and have had surgery to fuse vertebrae. Rehab involved a lot of very slow walking until I could walk for at least an hour. There were times when I really did not want to walk. It was hard and painful, and I felt like having a pity party for myself. *Lord, why me? I've been trying to serve You with all my heart, and now I have to go through this. Why do I have to go through this?* You know the routine, right? It's where our minds want to go when we're feeling sorry for ourselves.

But I remember going on a rehab walk, listening to some worship songs, and getting to a point when I pulled out my earplugs and just started thanking God. I told Him how grateful I was, quoted verses, and prayed for people. I prayed for my family, people I work with, our ministry, our city, people and churches who have ministered to me, people and churches I've had the privilege to minister to, and much more. All of a sudden I realized that it was one of the best times of praying that I'd had in several years. And it only happened because I had to walk when I didn't want to.

God doesn't expect you to manufacture feelings or go through the motions. But if you get started with Him in prayer, He will meet you there, and very often you will find a joy in those prayers that you would not have otherwise experienced, especially as you pray with gratitude. Whatever you're going through is not an accident, and it's absolutely not beyond God's reach. You can develop an upward focus by giving thanks in your prayers and choosing to fill them with joy.

An Attitude

Paul says he is confident that God will continue the work He began in the Philippians until its completion (v. 6). Choosing to be confident in what God is doing and what He has promised is absolutely critical for developing an upward focus.

A skeptic in Philippi might have called Paul out on this. After all, it didn't look like God was completing the work He started in Paul, or least with the visible side of his ministry. Paul had been busy traveling around the empire until he went back to Jerusalem and was suddenly arrested. From all appearances, things weren't working out very well for him.

Thankfully, Paul didn't look at life through a temporal lens. He saw everything through the lens of eternity. Even if life seems to be completely out of control, God is still in control. He works all things together for the good of those who love Him and are called according to His purpose (Rom. 8:28). From an eternal perspective, we have every reason to be confident in what He is doing and how our circumstances will work out.

My rehab walks gave me an opportunity to look back over my life with a different perspective than I had when I was going through hard times. That happens as you get older; things begin to look different. I realized, looking back over some of my hardest and most painful seasons, how powerful and sustaining it is to anchor in God's promises and His character.

I recently pulled out some of the packets of memory verse cards that I'd used so often early in my Christian life. I found one from 1978 called "God's Promises for Chip and Theresa." I wrote them about a month before we got married. One of them was an Old Testament passage that promised a good future. As I thought about the future that lay in front of me at the time I wrote that passage down, and how it actually turned out, I realized that my life was about a hundred times better than I could have dreamed. When we begin to focus on God's faithfulness, we're filled with confidence.

If you want to grow in your confidence in God's faithfulness, read the story of Joseph. It's the longest story in Genesis—the last thirteen chapters out of fifty—because it shows how a sovereign God brings good out of evil in a fallen world where things can go horribly wrong. Joseph was about seventeen when God gave him a promise, and for the next thirteen years, everything he went through made it look like that promise would never be fulfilled. He was rejected by his brothers and sold into slavery, falsely accused by his master and imprisoned, and forgotten for two years by the one person who might have been able to get him out. From a natural perspective, Joseph had every reason to think something was terribly wrong and God was no longer with him.

After thirteen years, God suddenly turned events in a direction that showed how everything Joseph had been through was actually moving him closer to the fulfillment of the promise, not away from it. Toward the end of the book, he said something to his brothers that has become a landmark statement about God's goodness and how He works out His purposes in our lives: "You meant evil against me, but God meant it for good" (Gen. 50:20). I don't profess to know how that works—how God can account for bad situations even before they happen and use them to fulfill His plans and promises—but He does. Even when we've made horrible mistakes, or people have done horrible things to us, we can be fully confident in His faithfulness toward us.

> There's nothing wrong with feelings, but they are not our reality, and we don't have to obey them.

That's why our gratitude, our joy, and our confidence are never dependent on our circumstances. They are dependent on God's faithfulness, which remains constant regardless of anything we might go through. You can be grateful, prayerful, and confident of the future, not because you've got it all together or because you think your circumstances are going to change (though they very often will), but because God put His Spirit within you, and He who began a good work in you is going to see you through. That's His promise.

If you think about it, the very worst thing that could happen to us is death, which for a believer means being in the presence of Christ with no more problems or pain forever. So, if the worst that can happen to us leads to something wonderful, what do we have to fear? Please do not hear that last sentence as some trite spiritual platitude. It's true and it's real! No circumstances can steal our joy. That glorious future is our baseline, and anything else we receive is just an added blessing. Because our hope is not in this world, nothing the world throws at us can steal our hope. We live above fears and threats. Confidently.

Summary

If you don't feel grateful, joyfully prayerful, or confident, here's the good news: Our feelings always follow our focus. We don't choose our focus according to our feelings; we choose our focus regardless of our feelings, and the feelings will come.

This perspective goes against what most people have been taught in the last few decades. This generation has been brought up to believe that whatever we feel is our reality, and therefore we need to arrange our circumstances to produce or confirm the feelings we think we ought to have. There's nothing wrong with feelings, but they are not our reality, and we don't have to obey them. Just as eating junk food for momentary pleasure undermines our desire for long-term health, satisfying immediate feelings can draw us away from an ultimately satisfying life.

Jesus set the example for us on that issue. He didn't feel like dying on the cross. In fact, He even asked the Father if there was a plan B, any other way that might fulfill His purposes (Matt. 26:39). He defied His momentary feelings for a much greater goal—our salvation—which could not have been accomplished otherwise. He was also able to look past His immediate feelings for a much more lasting attitude, the one we are discussing in this book. He endured the cross "for the joy set before Him" (Heb. 12:2). He knew which feelings would distract Him from His mission and which would propel Him in it.

Did you catch the significance of that? Jesus knew that if He did not succumb to the feelings He felt in the moments before the cross, He would know everlasting joy. Joy involves feelings, but it goes much deeper than the up-and-down emotions we experience moment by moment. It's deep and lasting, and it does not depend on our circumstances. God wants us to experience authentic, fulfilling emotions. He doesn't want us to be ruled by feelings that contradict the truth.

Emotions are a beautiful gift from God; but our feelings do not define reality or provide a trustworthy guide for our decisions. We live in a day when people's internal feelings and perspective have triumphed over what God's Word says about what is true, right, and God's will for our lives. Feelings are a product of our thinking and the perspective that we bring in processing the various circumstances, trauma, health issues, and pain that we experience. Jesus refused to let His emotions dictate His behavior when the will of God was clearly opposed to what He felt. We must all learn to do the same.

THREE OBSERVATIONS

In Philippians 1:3–6, Paul has shown us how we can develop an upward focus. Then in verses 7–11, he demonstrates an outward focus. Three things in verses 7–8 have been both helpful and convicting to me in understanding what this outward focus implies.

Difficult Circumstances Reveal Our True Affections

Remember Bobby in the previous chapter? After the first fire that burned down his warehouse, he was depressed because he lost his possessions. He was a believer, but he had gotten caught up in all the trappings of money and prestige. But after the second fire, he had a different set of affections. He was a changed man, focused on his family and his workers, and even though the loss of his possessions hurt, it didn't devastate him.

Our ministry has a partnership with an organization called Steiger International that reaches the global youth culture, particularly young people who have little religious background or have walked away from their Christian upbringing. They have workers in more than one hundred global cities and go into areas that most Christians avoid. They see young people from all over the world come to Christ and grow as disciples. I did a one-week training in Germany for their staff, and then we met with some of their regional leadership teams. It was an amazing experience. I learned as much or more from them as they did from me.

I will never forget meeting Angela, the leader of the Ukraine team, a very committed and determined woman who decided to remain in Ukraine when its war with Russia broke out. There was a brief window of time when Angela was able to get her parents and her older children to the United States, but Angela and her teenage daughter stayed because they didn't want to leave while the country was being bombed and people were entering eternity without Christ. Her husband, leading the work in Poland, provided ongoing support as they transferred supplies from Poland to Ukraine at great risk. It wasn't hard to see where her affections were directed toward the gospel and her country. The extreme hardship she endured made that clear. What impressed me, as much or more than her sacrifice, was her joy, and how God was reaching so many in the midst of all the chaos. Her parents and grown children were safely in the US, while she and her teenage daughter and husband were more concerned about the eternal future of the people in Poland and Ukraine than they were for their own safety.

We Can Live Above Our Circumstances

Living above our circumstances occurs when our hearts are so full of people there is no room for self-pity. That's what happened with Bobby after his second fire. Within a couple of days, he had helped all twelve of his master craftsmen to find jobs with his competitors.

When people are squeezed like a sponge, you find out what is really inside them. Paul was squeezed by persecution and imprisonment, and it became clear that he loved God with all his heart and cared deeply about people. The Philippians sent money and expressions of concern to Paul, and Paul responded with concern for the Philippians because he had an outward focus.

You can learn a lot about yourself when you face pressure and problems. Whatever oozes out of you, that's what is going on inside. If you're negative, critical, and blaming, your focus is off. I know because I'm guilty of this. With all the problems with my back and the surgeries I went through, I turned inward at times. I'll never forget a comment my wife made as I was rehabbing my second back surgery. We were sitting in the living room, and Theresa asked if I realized how negative I'd become recently. At first I reacted defensively, but she went on.

> **You can learn a lot about yourself when you face pressure and problems.**

"You know I love you, and I know you're in pain," she said. "But everywhere we go, we talk about your back, and you tell people a long story about everything that is going on with it. Your focus has become all about you and it sounds like you're complaining."

I had to admit, it was true. So I drew a smiley face on an index card, wrote "Lighten Up" next to it, and then wrote out Philippians

4:4–5: "Rejoice in the Lord always; again I will say, rejoice! Let your gentle spirit be known to all men. The Lord is near." Underneath that, I wrote, "Be positive! Be thankful! Don't seek sympathy!" And I've been practicing that daily as I made it the bookmark in my Bible.

We easily form negative habits in our attitudes and words. Before we know it, we're being critical, judgmental, pessimistic, and self-focused. It's easy to have a great attitude when everything is going great, but we're called to something higher and deeper: a positive, upward, outward focus even when things are challenging.

God Allows Adverse Circumstances to Realign Our Affections

In that season of my physical pain and recovery, God revealed some of my blind spots, and for that I'm thankful. Sometimes our self-focus keeps us looking inward, and we miss what He wants us to see. Whenever we go through difficulty, we face a strong temptation to think we've done something wrong or God doesn't love us anymore. It's true that He sometimes disciplines us through our circumstances, but more often He is using those circumstances to realign our affections away from some idol or unhealthy attachment.

> God loves us too much to leave us stuck in harmful affections.

When we can't find comfort or security in our circumstances anymore, we have to look to Him instead, which is exactly where He wanted us to look all along.

God loves us too much to leave us stuck in harmful affections. Sometimes in adversity we're praying, "Oh, God, take it away, take it away!" And He's saying, "No! My goal isn't to make your life comfortable. My goal is to give you lasting joy, and the only way you ever will really be happy is if you're holy. The only way to become holy is by recognizing what needs to be changed, asking Me to forgive, cleanse, and empower you through the discipline of hardship and discomfort." That's His desire for us, and it runs deeper than our immediate feelings and desires.

Summary

Our focus always follows our affections. By "affections," I don't mean the fleeting feelings we discussed earlier. Feelings tend to follow our focus. But our focus reveals our true affections—our values and interests, or where we've invested our hearts. For much of my life, I've directed my affections at being productive because, deep inside, I believed productivity is what made me valuable to God and people—not entirely, but that lie has been one I've battled all my life. That was one of my blind spots that God revealed through adversity, and that core belief or affection determined my focus.

If you want to know the affections that determine your focus, you can pick up some big clues in your calendar and credit card statements. Where are you directing your time and money? If you play golf seven days a week, you can probably say that your affection for golf has made that your focus. If you work seventy hours a week, perhaps your affection for productivity is driving you. If you wake up in the morning thinking about bank balances and stock market fluctuations, your focus is being shaped by an affection for financial status and security. That's just how it works. We focus on what we love and believe is important.

I'm sure you can see the implications for your spiritual life. This is why Jesus urged people to seek first the kingdom of God and trust that God would take care of everything else (Matt. 6:33). When you go through adversity, God is not down on you. He will use that adversity to redirect you. That doesn't mean He orchestrates your challenges and difficulties—we do have an enemy and live in a world that is hostile to God and His people, after all. In a fallen world, disasters and tragedies happen. But He will use those challenges and difficulties for good. The issue is how you respond to adversity and what you focus on as you're going through it.

SHIFTING YOUR FOCUS OUTWARD

At this point, you may be thinking, *Okay, Lord. I want to choose joy, and I understand that I need to have an upward and outward focus. But how do I get there?*

We've talked about learning how to develop an upward focus through thankfulness, prayer, and confident trust, and we've seen how adversity can reveal what's in our hearts and help us realign our affections. But developing an outward focus is a little different. How do we get to the point that we pray for people the way Paul did, even when we're under pressure?

Paul gives us the answer to those questions in Philippians 1:9–11, and it all has to do with our thinking.

Think About Those Who Have Loved You the Most

Paul already expressed that in verse 3. He thanked God for the Philippians, who had just shown their support with financial help and a visitor to check on him. He was entirely dependent on visitors for food, personal needs, and emotional support, and the Philippians had shown that they were willing to provide in whatever way they could.

Pray for Those You Think About the Most

Some of us spend a lot of time thinking about the people who have offended us most. It's better to think about those who have loved us the most and pray for them as we think about them. And if you can pray for those who have offended you, without dwelling on the offense, do that too.

Not all prayer is the same. I had a friend years ago named Ben who struggled with his focus—a glass-half-empty guy, even when the glass was mostly full. I tried to help him see that, and one time I asked him if he prayed about those things he was struggling with.

"Yeah, I pray," he said. "It doesn't help."

> **He didn't pray at all. He just whined in the presence of God.**

"Well, let's pray right now," I suggested.

We got on our knees, and he started. "God, You know the terrible childhood I had. You know how bad my father was, how other kids teased me all my life, how I can't hold down a job, no one likes me, and ..." He went on and on like this with everything that had gone wrong. It was all about his grievances. He didn't pray at all. He just whined in the presence of God.

I had to say something. "Excuse me, can I cut in here?"

He stopped and waited.

"Lord, please help Ben. Amen." Then I asked him, "Is that how you normally pray?"

"Yeah, I guess so."

"Ben, I've got news for you. You can pray what you were praying all day long and God is not going to answer that. It isn't even prayer. You're just telling God about everything you don't like." I pointed out that he had told me and a lot of other people in the congregation the same things several times.

"Have you noticed that when you come around, other people start going away?" I asked him.

"Yeah, it's terrible, isn't it?"

"Ben, there's a reason. You're like a track stuck on repeat. All you do is whine and complain. We've tried to help, but you keep going back to the same broken record."

I suggested we try a different kind of prayer, and he agreed.

"Lord, would You help Ben see You like he's never seen You before? Would You help him understand who You are and know how much You love him? Would You give him discernment about what's true and what isn't so he can approve the things that are excellent and be, like Paul prayed, 'sincere and blameless until the day of Christ'?"

We prayed all the same things Paul prayed for the Philippians. Being "sincere and blameless" (1:10) presents a picture of being tested by sunlight and shown to be morally pure. The last line of this prayer gives the reason for the request. Paul refers to the Philippians as "having been filled with the fruit of righteousness" (v. 11). It's a passive perfect participle, which means it has happened in the past and continues on into the future.

These are things we can pray for our spouses, kids, coworkers, fellow believers, or anyone. It's fine to pray for people's felt needs and for God to help them in the trials they are going through, but sometimes we need to go further. Paul tells us in these verses specifically what he was praying for the people he cared about.

I love those prayers because I want God to answer them for the people I love. Here's how I pray for my adult children: "Lord, would You give them genuine, experiential knowledge of You so that they sense You and understand You like they never have before and know, as they walk through this world, not to be pulled in this or that direction, but only follow in the steps that You have laid out for them? Would You keep them pure in their hearts and minds and stir in them such a love for You that they would be the kind of men and women who honor You and reflect Your goodness to the people around them, including my grandchildren?" This is the gist of what Paul prayed for the believers at Philippi, and it's powerful because it's focused upward and outward for God's glory.

Here's another paraphrase of what Paul prayed in the first few verses of his letter to this church: "Philippians, it's a hard world, but let me tell you something. I'm praying that you would know God like never before. And I'm praying you'll get it so crystal clear that when you see all the trash and temptations this world gives you, you'll know this is not the way you want to go—that instead you would walk with God in such a way that shows what happened when you received Christ. The old person died, the Spirit of God came into your life, and the righteousness and its fruit that He purchased for you represents how God sees you now. It's not about trying hard to be a good person. You actually possess the righteousness of Christ and live out by faith what is already operating in you until the day Jesus returns."

That's a profoundly theological and personal prayer. If you start praying for people you care about that way, your self-pity will vanish. You may still ask God to help them sell their car, keep their house, or get a new job—there's nothing wrong with those requests—but you'll also be focused on God's even greater plan for their lives. You see, the goal is not just for God to make life easier or better. It's to make us more like Christ so that we become change agents, catalysts for transformation in the people and situations around us.

FOCUS TRANSFORMS LIVES

Well, we've covered a lot of ground in these first eleven verses of Philippians 1. Let's go back to that simple formula to help you put this upward and outward focus into perspective. Remember, C + P = E. Circumstance plus perspective equals experience. If you take perspective out of that equation, you'll end up disappointed, frustrated, depressed, and eventually disillusioned. If you remember how vital perspective is, you can choose joy in any season of life—even the hard ones.

So, let me ask you, what are you facing and where's your focus? What perspective will you choose to embrace?

Is your focus upward? *Lord, what do You want to do in and through this situation?*

Is it outward? *Lord, how do You want to use me in this situation? How can I meet others' needs and pray for them in their adversity?*

Those shifts in perspective will not only transform you; they can also transform the lives of people around you. And as your heart gets filled up with loving and trusting God and loving other people, you will experience joy—not because your circumstances suddenly changed, but because you are now seeing circumstances through the lens of God's truth rather than looking at life through the lens of circumstances.

Joy is the evidence of Christ's presence operating freely in your heart. It's a gift of the Spirit. God wants you to have it. And understanding the power of focus is the first step in filling your life with it.

Summary and Action Steps

- **THE DIVINE EQUATION: C + P = E**

  Circumstance + Perspective = Experience

- Key #1 is the Principle of Focus
- The Question to Ask Yourself = Where is my focus?
  - Upward?
  - Outward?
  - Inward?

DISCUSSION/APPLICATION QUESTIONS

1. How did you feel after reading this chapter? What bubbled up to the surface in your thoughts?

2. Which of the specific practices to develop an upward focus were most helpful to you? Why?

3. Which of the specific practices to develop an outward focus were most helpful to you? Why?

4. What specific step of obedience/faith do you sense God wanting you to take to develop an upward and outward focus in the midst of your current circumstances?

5. Who will you ask in the next twenty-four to forty-eight hours to help you keep that specific commitment and stay on track?

Assignment: Below is a copy of the card that I have reviewed for many months to begin renewing my mind and change my thinking. Write out on an index card what I have here, or personalize it for yourself, and then review it multiple times in the morning and before you go to bed. You'll be amazed at the difference.

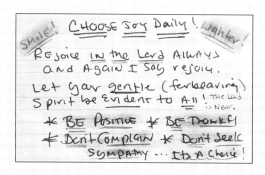

CHAPTER 3:

The Power of Purpose

The shortest distance between two points is a straight line." You probably learned that in geometry class. In the worlds of math and flat terrain, it's absolutely true. The distance between point A and point B is always a straight line.

But it isn't true in God's kingdom. In His economy, the shortest distance between two points—where you are and where He's taking you—is very often a zigzag.

I'll never forget the first time I heard that. It was in a message given by Don Sunukjian, a professor of preaching and Christian ministry. I don't remember exactly where I was or what the rest of the message was about, but I remember that statement because it sparked a paradigm shift for me. I realized that when I'm at point A and want to get to point B, I shouldn't be surprised by obstacles, detours, and struggles that seem to slow things down or take me in unexpected directions.

Like a lot of people, I thought very linearly then. I didn't always do a great job of handling barriers and delays. When I was single, I wondered when I would ever get married. When I was preparing for ministry, I wanted to get through as fast as I could in order to have the impact I wanted to have. In marriage, I wanted to get conflict resolved as quickly as possible. If there was a problem, I wanted to fix it. If there was a plan, I wanted to complete it. Getting from point A to point B seemed to be a simple proposition, and when it didn't turn out that way, I found it very frustrating.

So it was a huge relief when I realized that, in God's way of doing things, the journey almost always involves some twists and turns.

Paul would have agreed. God called him to take the gospel to the world—not only to Jews, but also (and especially) to gentiles—and as Paul went on missionary journeys and planted many churches, God used him greatly. But a lot happened between his point A (when God first spoke to him) and his point B (the fulfillment of his mission). He was redirected into Europe after trying to minister in Asia (Acts 16:6–10), thwarted from going places he wanted to go (1 Thess. 2:18), chased out of cities where he wanted to stay (Acts 16:39–40; 17:10–14; 20:3), and also beaten, stoned, imprisoned, shipwrecked, slandered, and in constant danger (2 Cor. 11:23–28). The path from calling to completion of his mission was not a straight one—or an easy one.

Now writing to the Philippians, Paul had been a prisoner for at least two and a half years and probably longer. He could easily have felt like he'd been put on the shelf for way too long. The most he could do was correspond with people and churches in his sphere of influence. So he wrote a few letters.

Of course, what might have looked relatively fruitless from Paul's perspective turned out to be a major strategic advance from God's perspective. Paul could not have known that his thirteen surviving letters would be included in Scripture and influence billions of people and entire civilizations over the next two thousand years. His zigzag circumstances turned out to be one of God's straight lines between calling and completion.

David is another example. God chose David to be king and had Samuel anoint him as Saul's successor, but Saul remained on the throne for years to come—more than a decade. Meanwhile, David had to dodge spears, hide in caves, contend with Israel's enemies, lose his wife, and deal with many other challenges as an increasingly deranged Saul pursued him around the countryside. David had to be wondering what that call to kingship was all about. Was it really God's plan for the anointed next king to barely escape attempts on his life for years?

David may not have realized it as a young man, but even though he had been anointed as the next king, he wasn't ready to be king yet. He had to be able to carry the weight of his calling, and several years in the wilderness—during which David admirably refused to rush God's plan—prepared him for the challenges of ruling God's people. To David, this had to look like a long, confusing zigzag. To God, it was the direct route into His plan.

We could say the same about many other biblical characters:

- Joseph, who we looked at in the last chapter, spent about thirteen years zigging and zagging away from the promise God had given him, only to find out that God had been moving him toward it all along.

- Moses spent forty years in Egypt and then another forty on the other side of a desert before he was ready to deliver the Israelites from their captivity.

- Israel as a nation had a winding history to enter into God's promises.

- Church history as a whole has hardly taken a straight line in fulfilling its mission.

In fact, we could make the case that almost everyone God has used powerfully to fulfill His purposes—whether in the Bible, later history, or our own time—has experienced disorienting delays and detours while, from God's perspective, walking straight into His higher and deeper plans.

> **You can choose joy even in the midst of a disorienting journey because God is using it.**

If you're in the middle of circumstances that make you wonder what in the world is going on, be encouraged by that. If anything in your life makes you think, *Lord, if You really love me, and if I'm really obeying You as I think I am, I don't understand why this is happening,* you aren't alone. You are traveling that path between point A and point B that doesn't look anything like a straight line from geometry class, but looks very much like the zigzag journey of God's people.

GOD'S PATH IN GOD'S TIMETABLE

You can choose joy even in the midst of a disorienting journey because God is using it. Even if He didn't orchestrate it—even if it's the consequences of your own mistakes or ungodly things people have done to you—He knew about it ahead of time, took it into account, and is accomplishing His purposes through it. I can't recall how many times I prayed and claimed out loud in my zigzag journey: "The LORD will accomplish what concerns me; Your lovingkindness, O LORD, is everlasting; Do not forsake the works of Your hands"

(Ps. 138:8). Don't be surprised if your path isn't linear. In fact, you should be surprised if it is. God almost always incorporates zigzags into His plans. It's just the way He works.

Paul understood this. He knew God's ways. His words to the Philippians reflect the wisdom and maturity of someone who had seen God work through life's zigzags again and again. As Paul described his circumstances and explained how God was using them, he deliberately chose to see the glass as half full. He had learned C + P = E, that circumstances plus perspective equals experience, and his perspective on everything he was going through was positive.

He also seemed to understand that the Philippians were not looking through the same lens. Some of them may have been discouraged, and some were struggling with the challenges the church was facing. Later in this letter, Paul told these believers how to train their minds not to be anxious and to think good, true, honorable, pure, lovely thoughts about what he and they are going through (4:4–9), but even in these first few verses, he demonstrated what that thought life looks like. He modeled the practice of focusing not on whatever is going wrong or lacking but on how God is at work for our good.

Nowhere in this letter did Paul blame God or people for his trials. He didn't deny his trials, but he wasn't focused on their negative effects. Despite the most serious challenges Paul faced, he chose joy.

We saw in the first two chapters how that choice involved looking through a certain lens. Key number one in living a life of joy is focus. And the key question when you're discouraged, confused, ticked off, or otherwise unhappy with the way things are going is: *Where is my focus?*

As we look at the next section of this letter (1:12–18), we see another key and another question that relates to it:

KEY #2: Purpose
Question #2: What is my purpose?

Key number two is *purpose*. And the question we need to ask as we look at all the ups and downs in life is, *What is my purpose?*

If we look at our challenges without knowing our purpose, we won't know how to interpret them and might easily be overwhelmed by the difficulties they present. Paul understood his purpose and how God works, and that understanding shows up in verse 12 as soon as he begins talking about his circumstances.

We might call this verse his thesis statement: "Now I want you to know, brethren, that my circumstances have turned out for the greater progress of the gospel" (Phil. 1:12).

The believers in Philippi had a close connection with Paul and loved him. He and his team (including Silas, Timothy, and Luke) had birthed this church on their first visit to the city, and the church considered him a friend and a brother. But their beloved apostle was now confined in Rome, and they knew prisoners in his circumstances had to fund their own food and housing.

So, they sent him a gift through Epaphroditus, who stayed with Paul for a while and got sick while he was there. After Epaphroditus recovered, Paul sent him back to Philippi with this letter, and immediately after greeting them and expressing his gratitude for them and his joy in their fellowship, he wanted to address their concerns. Above all, they should know that these challenges they had heard about were turning out for the greater progress of the gospel.

This term for "greater progress" means "advancement." In a military context, it's used for cutting down all the trees and clearing all the brush that would hinder the army's advance. Paul is saying here that his imprisonment, rather than being an obstacle itself, is helping clear away the obstacles preventing the spread of the gospel—literally, the "good news."

Sometimes even people who have been Christians a long time forget that the gospel is good news. It's not a mandate to live a certain way (although it will definitely change how we live) or a set of religious beliefs and practices. The first Christians weren't going all over the empire just telling people to change their morals. The gospel message is an announcement that Jesus came to earth as God incarnate to live a perfect life, die on the cross, be resurrected, and deliver us out of bondage to sin and into the freedom of eternal life with Him.

> He was called to advance the gospel, and because he knew this was his purpose, he interpreted everything through that lens.

From Paul's perspective, the good news was reaching ears that otherwise would not have heard it. Paul was called to reach gentiles with this gospel message—not a set of instructions about how to live, but a happy proclamation: "Great news! We all fall short, we've all sinned, but God has visited our planet and died in our place. Our sins are forgiven! Will you receive that amazing gift?" That's the gospel, and for people in Rome's inner circles to hear it, gospel-preaching people would need to be placed in their midst. As we will see, Paul saw himself as one of those messengers.

That's the bottom line under Paul's circumstances. He was called to advance the gospel, and because he knew this was his purpose, he interpreted everything through that lens. If God had been using him to advance the gospel through preaching, training disciples, and planting churches, He would continue to use him to advance the gospel through his imprisonment.

EXHIBIT A: THE GOSPEL GOES FORTH

Paul's claim that his circumstances were advancing the gospel might have raised some eyebrows, so after presenting his thesis, he launched into the evidence. As he described his experiences, he presented them as exhibit A, exhibit B, and exhibit C in support of his thesis statement.

In his first example, Paul showed specifically how his imprisonment had worked out for the progress of the gospel: "My imprisonment in the cause of Christ has become well known throughout the whole praetorian guard and to everyone else, and . . . most of the brethren, trusting in the Lord because of my imprisonment, have far more courage to speak the word of God without fear" (Phil. 1:13–14).

We tend to read the New Testament through a twenty-first-century lens and think ancient Romans were just hearing another religious message they could choose to receive or not. But it's a little more complex than that, and understanding the context sheds light on Paul's challenges.

In imperial Rome, emperors had absolute control. By Paul's time, the Roman Senate commonly conferred divine (or semi-divine) status on emperors and some members of their family, and this imperial cult was thoroughly interwoven with the complex network of Greek and Roman gods. Not to make sacrifices to the emperor—or to pagan gods on the emperor's behalf—could be considered treasonous except for those who had received an exemption, like Jews. People could worship whatever god(s) they wanted to worship in addition to the approved list, but the Roman state and culture put a lot of pressure on everyone to honor the sanctioned beliefs.

Into this religious mix stepped Jesus, who claimed to represent the only true God and, in fact, even *be* God in the flesh. Though He fulfilled Jewish prophecies, He was rejected by His own people. He died and rose from the dead, as witnessed by at least five hundred people, and told His followers to go into all the world to preach the forgiveness of sins and the removal of sin's barriers between God and humanity, and invite people into a personal relationship with this one true God.

> **Paul believed he was embedded in the empire's power center to declare the greatest truth this planet has ever heard.**

By the early AD 60s, the Jesus sect, called "the Way", had grown but was still a small sect on a vast and eclectic religious landscape. So how would God give His key messengers a platform to reach people with the unique message of the gospel? One way would be to plant this particular spokesman, an apostle called to preach to gentiles, within the subculture of Rome's government and military.

That's how Paul saw his imprisonment. He was strategically embedded into the power center of the empire. The "whole praetorian guard" and "everyone else" who knew he was there—Paul had a knack for making his presence known—also knew *why* he was there: for the gospel. Paul believed he was embedded in the empire's power center to declare the greatest truth this planet has ever heard.

He probably also saw an opportunity to improve the reputation of Christians in Rome. A lot of people in the Roman world were suspicious of Christians. The Christians often met privately, had strange practices like eating and drinking the flesh and blood of their Lord with "brothers and sisters" at their "love feasts" (rumors of cannibalism and incest grew out of this terminology), were considered antisocial or treasonous for separating themselves from imperial religion, were willing to touch people with leprosy and other diseases, praised God even when being marched off to fight lions in the arena, and kept talking about a dead man who came back to life. A couple years after Paul likely wrote Philippians, Nero deflected responsibility for the Great Fire of Rome (AD 64) by blaming Christians for it, and he sometimes executed Christians who would not recant their faith by burning them as human torches in his gardens. Most people were not that hostile to Christians but simply thought they were weird.

Paul's imprisonment was a chance to change those perceptions among some powerful, influential people. He had the ear of members of the praetorian guard, who were assigned rotating shifts in guarding him for hours at a time. These were elite soldiers assigned to the special force surrounding the emperor, his family, senators, and other members of Roman government. Praetorian guardsmen numbered in the thousands—perhaps as many as twelve to fifteen thousand at times—to inhibit the potential for military coups and assassination attempts. Because Philippi was a Roman colony where many ex-military men retired, some members of the church likely had sons or nephews in the guard and would have been particularly interested in Paul's influence among guardsmen. Paul's influence in those circles could significantly advance the gospel and change the reputation of Christians. We can imagine that many guards, having been "captive" to Paul for hours at a time while holding him captive, were persuaded to accept Christ.

That shines a different light on his imprisonment, doesn't it?

The Philippians may have assumed it was a huge setback for his ministry and the advance of the gospel, but Paul assured them that it was just the opposite. This "zigzag" had a very straightforward and positive purpose.

You can probably point to several "negative" events in your life that have had positive effects too. Those hard times may have been much more strategic than you thought when you were going through them.

Are you going through a difficult time right now? If so, you may not be able to see how God wants to use it to advance His purposes—in your life or someone else's—but that will probably become clear if you respond to the pain or injustice with an attitude of joy and hope. God wants to use your present circumstances, as He did with Paul, for the furtherance of the gospel.

As wonderful as it is to recall Paul's story and hear his testimony, there's something deeply powerful about hearing firsthand how God uses adversity for good to our friends and fellow followers, who are trusting Jesus in the midst of their pain, disappointment, or health issues.

I was struck deeply by a conversation I had with Martha just a few weeks ago. She's one of our ministry partners and I called just to say thanks for her support of the ministry. I didn't know her personally, didn't know much about her, and before I could get thanks out of my mouth, she began to launch into a story and profusely thank me and our team for the frequent calls, the prayers, the teaching of God's Word that sustained her on this second bout with breast cancer.

I listened as she recounted a joy she couldn't explain as God has used her attitude in the midst of dire circumstances to let doctors, nurses, and staff at the hospital see and learn about Jesus. "As painful and difficult as it has been," she said, "it has been an amazing privilege to see the doors that have opened and watch faces light up as they hear and see the power of Jesus in my life."

I can't quite describe how I felt when I got off the phone. Here was someone battling a second round with cancer. Because of my experience with Theresa's cancer years ago, this hit close to home. I know what it's like to go through all those treatments and wonder whether your mate, or someone you love dearly, is going to live. My call intended to thank her turned into a moment of deep encouragement for me. The joy in her voice and the focus she had on others reminded me once again that C + P = E. Her perspective and example actually changed mine.

EXHIBIT B: THE CHURCH GROWS STRONG

Not only did God advance the gospel through Paul's imprisonment, He also strengthened the church through it. This is how Paul describes exhibit B: "Most of the brethren, trusting in the Lord because of my imprisonment, have far more courage to speak the word of God without fear" (Phil. 1:14).

In an age when the church in Rome was being persecuted and churches in other Roman cities were under a lot of pressure, Paul's example of enduring and even thriving under injustice emboldened Christians in any oppressive circumstances. If Paul could continue to have a strong testimony in those conditions, so could they.

I have a number of friends with high-level jobs in technology companies like Apple, Google, Intel, and Meta (formerly Facebook), and they are not afraid to identify themselves as Christians. They aren't asking permission regarding what they can and cannot say. They are loving, kind, and professional, yet they are also bold enough to be who they are without apologies—not anti-intellectual, narrow-minded "haters," but compassionate, considerate believers willing to talk about their faith and values. When people see how these men and women can be uncompromising in their beliefs while treating people with honor and respect, they are encouraged to do the same. They see a clear picture of it and think, *Yes, I can do that too.* You would likely be shocked at the number of Bible studies and prayer groups operating in these companies and many others because of the kind, bold, loving witnesses, and the experience of their work.

Sometimes adversity builds up the body of Christ. We might think it would have the opposite effect—that difficult circumstances create setbacks and cause people to shy away from their faith—but adversity often strengthens committed believers by clarifying their focus and reinforcing their resolve.

> When people see how these men and women can be uncompromising in their beliefs while treating people with honor and respect, they are encouraged to do the same.

One of my deepest, most difficult zigzags made things very clear for me. I had the privilege of leading Walk Thru the Bible for several years, and I loved that organization's mission and what it was accomplishing around the world. But as my administrative responsibilities increased, my opportunities to study, preach, and teach decreased. I was creating one or two videos a year and traveling around the world sharing them with other leaders who would teach the same material to others, but I wasn't in my sweet spot. I wasn't digging in and using the teaching and preaching gifts I had been given. The role became 15 percent creation and 85 percent distribution and fundraising. My joy was diminishing and my soul was shrinking.

"I want you to leave that role and go back to the local church," I sensed God tell me. So, I came up with a good transition plan that allowed time for me to find a job and leave Walk Thru the Bible in a good position. But that wasn't enough.

"No, I didn't tell you to set up a long-term plan," I felt God said. "I want you to resign."

My joy was diminishing and my soul was shrinking.

"But Lord, You don't understand. I don't have a job yet."

"I know. So do you trust Me or not?"

Whenever you find yourself telling God that He doesn't understand the situation, prepare to be redirected. He understands perfectly well and often prefers to put you in a position of believing before understanding.

I figured there would be some churches out there that needed a pastor like me, and I'm sure there were, but that wasn't God's immediate plan. For two years, I did not pastor a church. Living on the Edge was developing as an independent organization, and I was in limbo. I'd wake up every day and go to a little makeshift office with a handful of other employees and wonder if we were going to be able to pay the bills that month. I'd visit different churches on Sunday mornings, which I loved doing, but while I sat and listened, I questioned what God was doing and why He hadn't yet put me back in my sweet spot of teaching and preaching in a local church. In the middle of the process, I didn't have the perspective to see how God was deepening me while also preparing a church so that both I and the church would be ready to connect in ministry.

It would be easy to think that those two years were wasted, but a lot happened in that season that set the stage for greater impact. We did a lot of praying; the internet grew greatly in those years, expanding opportunities for communicators, and we eventually realized that Living on the Edge was not just a radio ministry or a teaching ministry, but also a platform for discipleship. We were on more than one thousand radio outlets reaching more than one million people weekly. We had morning time slots in the ten largest American cities and realized we needed to shift our focus from "How many people are listening?" to "How many people are growing into reproducing disciples?" It was a radical change and meant we had to move people from being listeners to connecting in discipleship groups in their areas. We were able to develop small-group material and launch small groups through the radio and later digitally. We developed more than twenty small-group resources used by millions of Christians and churches all around the world. Much of what we have done since then took shape during those two years, and it would not have happened if I had been employed full-time at a church.

> Paul got to a place we all need to get to: "Lord, my calling is Yours, my reputation is Yours, and my circumstances are Yours."

That was a zigzag that sharpened our focus. It wasn't easy, and even though it seemed like two years of just being frustrated and second-guessing what God was doing, He was doing more in this season to advance the gospel and strengthen His church than I could have done as pastor of a church or even a hundred churches.

God knows where you are and what you're going through. You may have times of being frustrated and doubting whether God is doing anything at all, but you can trust that He is. If you are not in the midst of a clearly fruitful season, He is setting you up for one.

EXHIBIT C: THE BELIEVER GROWS DEEP

Third, God not only uses our circumstances to advance the gospel and strengthen the church, He also gets very personal to help us grow deeper roots in Him.

That was one of the effects of my two-year season of frustration. It set up our ministry to help strengthen the church, but it also strengthened me in the process. Paul expressed deep spiritual maturity in describing how other preachers were filling the void left by his imprisonment. In exhibit C, Paul made his case for how God furthers His purposes in our adversity. Paul demonstrated how he had rooted himself in the calling God had given him, and his selfless desire to see the truth advance.

> Some, to be sure, are preaching Christ even from envy and strife, but some also from good will; the latter do it out of love, knowing that I am appointed for the defense of the gospel; the former proclaim Christ out of selfish ambition rather than from pure motives, thinking to cause me distress in my imprisonment. What then? Only that in every way, whether in pretense or in truth, Christ is proclaimed; and in this I rejoice. (Phil. 1:15–18)

Certain Christian teachers in Paul's day looked at his imprisonment with satisfaction. Believe it or not, people in ministry can operate in a competitive spirit sometimes, and apparently Paul's critics saw his circumstances as evidence that God had put him on the sidelines so they could expand their ministries. Some carried on in love and goodwill, understanding that preaching the gospel came with certain dangers. But others, out of "envy and strife," may have assumed that if Paul was in prison, he couldn't be God's man of the moment. After all, God blesses people who are walking in His will, and if Paul wasn't being blessed, then perhaps he wasn't the leader he was supposed to be. And they were happy to promote themselves in his absence as the new leaders in the church, God's spokesmen who were free and experiencing God's favor.

That must have been hard for Paul, not because of any ego or competitive nature, but because some people whom he had probably discipled were now betraying him or following self-centered preachers. His reputation was under assault even by fellow believers. Yet Paul remained focused on his purpose. What did God call him to do? He had been sent on a mission to take the gospel to the world and disciple people to be more like Jesus. If he was doing that wherever he was, he was fulfilling his calling, no matter what others were saying about him.

So, Paul simply pointed out that there were good motives and bad motives at work, but as long as Christ was being preached, what did it matter to him? His purpose was to get the name of Christ and the truth of the gospel out there, and even if some people were doing that in a self-centered way, his purpose was still being fulfilled. Remembering his purpose kept him grounded and took him deeper with God.

You have to grow deep to have that perspective. We sometimes assume that Paul was higher and holier than the rest of us, a stained-glass saint from the start, but there are no superstars in the body of Christ. He could have felt as competitive and resentful as anyone—if he let himself. But he refused to play the part of a victim. He may have had to wrestle with the unfairness of his situation and the people slandering him, but ultimately he wanted God to accomplish in him whatever God wanted to accomplish.

Paul got to a place we all need to get to: "Lord, my calling is Yours, my reputation is Yours, and my circumstances are Yours. What You think of me is more important than what anyone else thinks of me. Have Your way in my life." But not many people get there without some kind of pain or adversity.

We all have stuff to deal with, don't we? It can be anything—a dreaded diagnosis, an unreliable or unfaithful mate, a child going through an intense situation, a battle with anxiety or depression, a season of rejection, disappointment, or a terrible injustice. Whatever the case, you may find yourself in situations when life is not how you want it to be, and every day is a struggle.

Whenever your glass seems to be half empty, remember what you have. God is with you and has a purpose for your life. Claim and pray Psalm 138:8. Cling to that purpose and trust everything to Him. You'll find that even in those painful, challenging times, He is transforming you and growing you deep.

I have a close friend dealing with a physical issue that keeps him from driving, which makes it very difficult to run his business. His doctors have tried everything and haven't found a treatment that works. When I spend time with this friend, I ask him how he's really doing deep down inside.

"You know, the Lord is teaching me a lot," he says. "My wife gets up at five every morning to drive me to my job sites, and we have a great time together. And I've seen some things about myself that I don't like and that I don't think I would have seen if I hadn't been going through this."

He understands that God's purpose is to make him like Jesus. He doesn't like what he's going through, but he doesn't complain because he knows it's worth it. His attitude makes me want to be like Jesus.

When you are going through difficult, pressure-filled times and feel angry and tired and ready to give up, ask this question: *Lord, what do You want to do in me?* You may also ask how He wants to use this situation to help other people or grow His church, but don't forget His purposes within you as part of His plan. If you haven't discovered this already, you'll find that virtually everyone who has a deep relationship with God has been through a lot of adversity. That's when roots grow deep. Don't miss out on what He is doing. Don't waste your pain. Look at all of life through the lens of purpose.

DISCUSSION/APPLICATION QUESTIONS

1. Is there any circumstance you're facing right now that causes you to question God's love or concern for you?

2. Can you think of a time in your past when what you were going through didn't make sense, but later turned out to be a great blessing?

3. How did Paul's focus on God's purposes being fulfilled rather than his own comfort or relief transform his perspective?

4. What three positive things occurred as a result of Paul's imprisonment (exhibit A, B, C)?

5. How might God want to use your current circumstances to reach the lost, build up the body of Christ, or transform your life?

Assignment: Ask God to reveal what purposes He wants to accomplish through your present challenges. Write out Psalm 138:8 on an index card and thank God that He will, in His way and His time, fulfill what concerns you.

> The LORD will accomplish what concerns me;
> Your lovingkindness, O LORD, is everlasting;
> Do not forsake the works of Your hands.
> (Psalm 138:8)

CHAPTER 4:

How to Embrace Your Purpose

I was still playing a lot of pickup basketball with college guys when I was around forty, and I was still in pretty good shape. One misty, rainy Sunday afternoon, I thought someone could get hurt if we played outside, so we went into the gym, and I was having a good day. I was in a rhythm, the shots were falling, and I felt great. As I was dribbling and setting up a vintage John Stockton bounce pass—Stockton was one of my heroes and known for his assists—I caught a glimpse of a guy on the other team who anticipated where I was going with it. So, I leaned in even harder and put all my weight into it, and suddenly we heard an explosion in the gym. Everything inside my knee that could blow up did blow up—ACL, MCL, meniscus. The X-rays weren't pretty.

After surgery, I found myself in physical therapy for weeks, and I learned early on that my therapist's father was an ardent atheist who hated Christians. She saw on my paperwork that I was a pastor. "So, you're one of them," she said. "My dad taught me to hate you guys." I started to think she might enjoy the pain she was going to put me through.

I prayed for the right opportunity to talk to her, and around the seventh or eighth appointment, one came up. "Okay, so what's with you?" she said.

"What do you mean?" I asked.

"I see your attitude and how you act, and you've gotten to know everybody in here. You're not like all the Christians my dad told me about."

"Do you really want to know?" I asked. "I mean really?"

She said she did.

"Your dad missed out. He doesn't know." And that's when I started to explain who Jesus was. She had been through some horrendous hardships—a single mom abandoned by her husband—and she opened up, moving more deeply and honestly each session. She asked lots of questions and over time we became good friends. I will never forget her first visit to our church. She listened intently and after the service began to meet real people who genuinely cared for her and her daughter. After several months of searching and seeking, she trusted Christ as her Savior. I had the privilege of baptizing her, and she began coming to church and sitting right up front with her little girl. She started bringing her friends, and some of them received Christ too. Over the course of a few months, this young woman's life turned completely around.

When I had recovered, I went back to playing basketball—with a brace. I'd lost my edge, especially my quick first step, and I couldn't jump much at all. I was a little bummed out, but I sensed God's voice giving me perspective on it all.

"Chip, do you think this relatively small challenge of a compromised knee is worth the eternal destiny of that young woman and her daughter?"

Yes, Lord, I thought. That was pretty awesome. Would I give a knee for that outcome? Absolutely. My circumstances, as painful and disappointing as they were in the moment, turned out for the furtherance of the gospel.

That was one of many situations in my life that felt devastating at the time, but it convinced me of how God uses our zigzags for His purposes. However, we can't experience the power of purpose if we don't know what our purpose is. That's the crucial question that goes with the second key to choosing joy.

To put that another way, you can't experience deep, lasting joy if you don't have a sense of purpose. Nor can you have a sense of purpose if you don't get a good grasp on what's really important and how you fit into God's plans.

So, if purpose is a key to joy, we need to ask some very important questions: *What is my purpose? Why was I created? What am I called to do? Do my priorities reflect the purpose God has given me?*

PAUL'S SENSE OF PURPOSE

As we've seen, Paul's purpose was to advance the gospel. It wasn't his highest priority, as he explains to the Philippians a little later. His all-consuming passion was to know Christ and be found in Him (Phil. 3:9–10)—in other words, to have a deep, meaningful, intimate relationship with Jesus.

But you can't really know Christ deeply and intimately without wanting to make Him known, and in terms of outward ministry, this was the calling God had given Paul. As he implied in his "thesis statement" of Philippians 1:12, his purpose was to further the gospel, and his difficult circumstances were accomplishing that goal.

At a foundational level, advancing the gospel is our purpose too—in the world, among the body of Christ, and within ourselves.

And because we see how the zigzags in Paul's life furthered his mission, we can trust that God will use the zigzags in our lives to further our mission too. What He is calling us to do may require a deeper level of character and faith than we currently have, and as we saw in the last chapter, the zigs and zags are part of His loving agenda to make Christ known, strengthen His church, and deepen our faith. His ultimate purposes for our lives are often achieved by circumstances that seem to make no sense on the surface, but are accomplishing a significant work in us and through us. He is always advancing the good news of the gospel through His people to render its full effect in the world, the church, and our lives.

His ultimate purposes for our lives are often achieved by circumstances that seem to make no sense on the surface

---

I was talking with someone recently about places in the world that are very resistant to the gospel. One of the reasons so many people oppose that message is that they know how powerful it is. When people in hard-to-reach and often dangerous places receive Jesus, everything changes. They can see how different God's kingdom is from what they knew before, and they are radically transformed. I am humbled as I rub shoulders with believers who have come to Jesus from atheistic, communist, or radical Islamic environments where the cost of converting to Christianity is imprisonment or death.

Those of us who live in countries where churches are practically everywhere don't always get that. We risk getting so familiar and comfortable with the gospel that we forget how radical it is. As our culture increasingly looks down on believers, we may also get quieter about what we believe because we don't want to deal with the consequences of being completely open about it. Without meaning to, we begin to devalue the message that has changed our lives.

People who have lived far from God, stuck in enslaving addictions, crushed by a sense of futility or brokenness, or who have simply felt lost and hopeless as long as they can remember don't have to be convinced of the power of the gospel once they've received it. They remember what life was like before they received Christ and how different it is afterward.

New Testament believers were not transformed by some ethereal experience or vague belief in eternal life. They were transformed by the Jewish Messiah who fulfilled hundreds of prophecies and was raised from the dead as verified by living eyewitnesses (1 Cor. 15:3–8). He dramatically appeared to Paul (Acts 9:1–19), and Paul's life was radically and permanently changed. No one had to convince Paul that the

> **Without meaning to, we begin to devalue the message that has changed our lives.**

advance of the gospel was a foundational priority or that the gospel message was powerful. As he had written to the Roman church a few years before he arrived in Rome, "I am not ashamed of the gospel, for it is the power of God for salvation to everyone who believes, to the Jew first and also to the Greek" (Rom. 1:16). Even as a prisoner in Rome, he knew God was accomplishing His purposes.

Remember, one of Paul's purposes in writing to the Philippians was to encourage this small church to keep the faith and choose joy. He wanted them to experience the fullness of joy that God promises, and he began by redirecting their focus. He demonstrated that "circumstances plus perspective equals experience," that is, C + P = E. He then demonstrated the power of understanding our purpose. He understood that God had given him an unusual assignment and that his mission was not exactly like anyone else's, but he also knew he shared the same fundamental purpose with every other believer. By focusing on that purpose early in his letter to the Philippian church, Paul reminded his readers (and us) to look at life through that lens.

I believe we can discern from this passage three purpose statements that are true for all of us. They aren't just for people with a calling like Paul's or some special gift to preach or teach. They're for everyone. God may point out more specific purposes for you—what we might call a particular calling or assignment—but whatever that mission is, it will somehow fit into these larger purpose statements. Before you move on to anything more specific, you'll need to make sure these are foundational in your life.

Purpose Statement #1: I Am an Ambassador/Messenger of the Gospel

The good news of the gospel won't go anywhere in your relational network if it doesn't come through you. You are strategically placed in your family and where you live and work to represent the gospel with your life and your words. The people around you may be good family members, friends, neighbors, and coworkers, but many of them are lost. They need to know Jesus and experience the power of the gospel.

Purpose: Reach the "lost"
Question #1: How can God use my circumstances to advance the gospel?

I grew up in the United States but had no idea what the gospel was. I would not have become a Christian if someone had not shared it with me. If one of your foundational purposes is to be a messenger of the gospel, what are you doing about it? How are you living out and talking about that message?

Paul had a lot of glass-half-full experiences: seeing people receive his message with joy, seeing people healed through his prayers and his touch, and speaking to key leaders around the Mediterranean world to advance the kingdom of God. However, he also had many glass-half-empty experiences of beatings, imprisonments, rejection, shipwreck, and more, and yet he chose to see what God was doing in them.

In everything we go through in life, we need to see through that lens of purpose. *How is God's agenda being accomplished? How are His promises being fulfilled? Beyond my current comfort level, what is He doing through me and in my circumstances to reach human hearts and transform lives?*

Not everyone asks these kinds of questions. Many people in our times have been brainwashed from an early age to live for weekends and holidays and get as much as we can so we can retire at an early age and enjoy life. These messages are ingrained in us through consumerism, advertising, entertainment, career counseling, and the culture at large. One of our society's highest values is self-actualization—becoming all you want to be, getting all you want to get, and doing all you want to do in order to feel fulfilled.

It is considered admirable to search for meaning in life, but you might be ridiculed if you claim to have found it in Jesus. Our culture applauds those who are "making a way for themselves" or "trying to make a difference" (without defining what that difference is) from a limited, earthbound perspective, but looks down on those who are investing their lives in eternity. It commends selfless acts of kindness even while rewarding selfishness and me-focused lifestyles. "You be you" is an affirming mantra for almost everyone unless "you" happen to support biblical, sometimes called "traditional," values and/or commit your life to Jesus.

Paul saw himself and every other believer as an ambassador for Christ. He lived out his purpose and preached purpose to everyone who believed in Jesus. One of his great "purpose" passages can be found in 2 Corinthians, where, in defending his calling against his critics, he sets an example for all Christians to follow:

> For the love of Christ controls us, having concluded this, that one died for all, therefore all died; and He died for all, so that they who live might no longer live for themselves, but for Him who died and rose again on their behalf.
>
> Therefore from now on we recognize no one according to the flesh; even though we have known Christ according to the flesh, yet now we know Him in this way no longer. Therefore if anyone is in Christ, he is a new creature; the old things passed away; behold, new things have come. Now all these things are from God, who reconciled us to Himself through Christ and gave us the ministry of reconciliation, namely, that God was in Christ reconciling the world to Himself, not counting their trespasses against them, and He has committed to us the word of reconciliation.
>
> Therefore, we are ambassadors for Christ, as though God were making an appeal through us; we beg you on behalf of Christ, be reconciled to God. He made Him who knew no sin to be sin on our behalf, so that we might become the righteousness of God in Him. (2 Cor. 5:14–21)

One of your purposes is to be an ambassador and a messenger of the gospel in order to reach the lost—to present the message of reconciliation between God and humanity. And very often that message will speak the loudest when you are going through difficult circumstances. People usually don't receive the gospel simply from hearing about it. They receive it when they see it at work in someone's life. You may not see the full purpose in your adversity, but living in light of the gospel as someone reconciled to God fills every day with purpose no matter what you're going through.

People need to know that God has a great agenda to restore people through a relationship with Him. Plenty of people have been wounded by Christians and the church, and Christ is not always represented well in personal or public conversations, but Jesus loves you and everyone around you. People need to see that love regardless of their problems, character flaws, political views, past mistakes, dysfunction, or any other baggage they are carrying. They also need to know that in spite of all the existential threats, political turmoil, and social ills they see in today's news, they can be rooted and grounded in eternity through a relationship with Jesus.

> You are an ambassador of Christ and a messenger of the gospel that accepts people in love, gives them peace, and promises them joy—even when your circumstances or theirs preach a message that makes joy difficult.

Like Paul, you are an ambassador of Christ and a messenger of the gospel that accepts people in love, gives them peace, and promises them joy—even when your circumstances or theirs preach a message that makes joy difficult. In every situation, live and speak the greater message of what God has done and how He is advancing the good news.

Purpose Statement #2: I Am Called to Encourage God's People to Grow to Full Maturity

The second purpose every believer can claim is to encourage God's people and help them grow into full maturity. Followers of Jesus are exhorted in Hebrews 10:24–25 to "stimulate one another to love and good deeds" and encourage one another—to build each other up and spur each other on. Earlier in that letter we are told to encourage each other daily "so that none of you will be hardened by the deceitfulness of sin" (Heb. 3:13). God wants to use whatever we are going through to encourage our brothers and sisters and build up the body of Christ.

This is what Paul did in explaining how his trials were advancing the gospel and pointing out that his imprisonment had increased the boldness of many to speak the message without fear. Not only are we to reach "the lost"; we are also called to build up "the found." The question we need to ask ourselves is how God might use every circumstance, even our most difficult, to encourage other believers.

> **Purpose:** Build up the "found"
> **Question #2:** How can God use my circumstances to encourage other believers?

Again, this is not just Paul's purpose statement; it's ours. It applies to every single believer. No one grows in isolation. However much you've grown as a believer, you have done so because someone helped you. That's certainly true for me; many times, at many stages of life, I've been encouraged, nourished, challenged, and taught by people who had gifts from God that I needed to experience and words I needed to hear. I'm sure that's true of you too.

Think about who you are discipling. Who are you mentoring or coaching? Who is influenced by your words and examples? In what ways are you pouring your life into other people for their spiritual growth and well-being? Whether you want to or not, you do influence other people. Is your influence building them up? It's important to see this as a God-given purpose and be intentional about living it out.

This isn't as difficult or time-consuming as you might think. If you live with an upward and outward focus, much of it happens naturally. People will see you as an encouraging example as you trust God in the midst of adversity without turning inward and complaining about how difficult things are. Your focus and your purpose will demonstrate your faith and God's power at work in you. But there are also things you can do, like sending someone an affirming, encouraging email, walking with people through their crises and challenges, or giving appropriate, biblical counsel and advice when someone needs to hear godly wisdom on whatever they are dealing with. It's important to have specific discipling or mentoring relationships with some people, but encouraging other believers and spurring them on to good works often just happens as we live life and notice the opportunities.

> We've been conditioned to focus more on our rights than on other people's welfare.

Unfortunately, we won't notice those opportunities if we have an inward focus or don't understand our purpose to build up the body of Christ. Our culture has done us no favors on this point; many people have been taught to see themselves as victims and society itself as an oppressor, as if friends and family members, governments, schools, businesses, and other people in our lives owe it to us to make us feel the right way and have the right experiences, and we learn to blame someone when we don't. We've been conditioned to focus more on our rights than on other people's welfare. Scripture shows us another way, and the Holy Spirit empowers us to live with the selfless, sacrificial, relentless love of God in our relationships with others.

Spend some time thinking about how your current circumstances—whether they are "normal" or unusually difficult—could provide an opportunity to build up a brother or sister in Christ.

When our ministry was working with Walk Thru the Bible, we created multiple video resources for pastors and teachers in countries around the world to use however they needed. In the years following that partnership, we received numerous requests from leaders in other countries for renewed permission to use material, and we always gave it to them. Eventually, we realized that we needed a strategy and a plan. We determined that China and the Middle East were among the most strategic places to reach, and we already had some books, satellite programming, and relational networks that gave us a starting point in those two regions. China would be particularly challenging because of the way the government structures and limits the state-sanctioned church, and because of the scarce resources and education among leaders in non-sanctioned house churches. There are millions of Christians and thousands of church leaders in China, but many don't have any theological background nor the means to develop teaching resources to reach China's massive population. God let us target several major cities in China and partner with pastors to do teaching and training on core topics like "Who is God?" and "What is a disciple?" We made several trips to the mainland to teach in various cities in seminaries and to help pastors, who would then teach and train other pastors throughout the country. It was a train-the-trainer model and was extremely effective (2 Tim. 2:2).

After we had taken a number of trips and seen some amazing results, the government began to place restrictions on our activities. On one occasion just days before leaving for China, I received a message that our two days of training would be cut in half. I was to teach an eight-part series followed by small group time with sermon notes for Chinese pastors to teach in their churches throughout the country, and doing it in half the time would be impossible. The goal, I believe, was to discourage us from coming.

I didn't know what the Lord had in mind but determined that we would press ahead and do the very best we could with the time that we had. Then I remembered that on a former trip we had shown a brief teaching in English with Chinese subtitles at one of the events, and one of our translators who accompanied me from our church in California suggested that we put the translation at the top of the videos so people in the back of the room could see them better. I didn't think much of it at the time, but when we returned

> Tears were streaming down their faces. I realized that God in His "zigzag" sovereignty had provided a way for us to do training in half the time.

after that earlier trip, we translated all of our video training with Chinese subtitles at the top of the videos to give to key leaders for review when they would train other pastors after we left.

On the plane, the Lord gave me an idea. What if I did the first session or two live and built relationships with the pastors and then tested to see if showing the videos would work? It would cut our time in half because rather than me speaking and having it translated, everyone would get the material simultaneously on the video with the translation already available. The problem was, I didn't know if it would really work. Would the subtitles get the message across clearly and powerfully?

I will never forget the third session when I used the video. It was a teaching about the character of God and His sovereignty. I shared an illustration about some very painful times in my life and family where God sovereignly used some pain in the short term to bring about some good in the long term. As the pastors watched the video, I watched them. Tears were streaming down their faces. I realized that God in His "zigzag" sovereignty had provided a way for us to do training in half the time.

We eventually provided more than one million copies with training and sermon notes on the character of God prior to the close of the country with the pandemic. We also were able to print more than one million copies of a key resource on what it means to be a disciple according to Romans 12.

With every trip, the restrictions became tighter and tighter, and our ability to personally do the training became more limited. When the pandemic hit and the country completely closed, I was thrilled to see that the Chinese leaders took on the training themselves. The ultimate restriction of us not being allowed in the country did something even better; local leaders took over all the teaching and began to share with others what they had learned. Sometimes the most frustrating and difficult things that happen in our lives God uses for good. We see that when we remember to look through the lens of purpose. In this case, the more the restrictions, the more God provided creative alternatives and caused His church to be strengthened, just like the apostle Paul's challenges strengthened the body of Christ in his day.

Purpose Statement #3: I Am a Servant of the Living God

Whatever you're going through, no matter how good or bad it may be, you can be confident in at least one aspect of God's will for your life. Are you ready? Here is His will for you: to make you like Jesus.

That means that there will very often be something in your adverse circumstances that puts you in a position to serve. Jesus described His mission in terms of servanthood: "Even the Son of Man did not come to be served, but to serve, and to give His life a ransom for many" (Mark 10:45). He also told His disciples that when a pupil is fully trained, he will be like his teacher (Luke 6:40). In other words, you are being conformed to the image of a Master who humbly serves and lives sacrificially. Your adversity provides unique opportunities to do that.

So, the third purpose statement that every believer can claim is to become like our Master, and the question we need to ask is what God wants to do within us in every situation we face. The first two purpose statements were focused on what God wants to do *through* us; this one is focused on what He wants to do *in* us.

Purpose: Become like our Master
Question #3: What might God want to do in me through my present circumstances?

The psalmist who wrote Psalm 119 understood the connection between our challenging circumstances and God's work within us. He wrote, "Before I was afflicted I went astray, but now I keep Your word" (v. 67) and, "It is good for me that I was afflicted, that I may learn Your statutes" (v. 71).

This psalm doesn't identify its author, though David is traditionally thought to have written it. If so, he isn't talking about a few minor obstacles or speed bumps in his life. David spent years running for his life, was betrayed by family members and some of his closest friends, and experienced enormous grief during much of his life. He knew about adversity, and he knew from experience how he could stray from God's purposes. Difficulties kept him focused on God and His Word, and God used those difficulties to develop and strengthen his character and faithfulness.

God is not the author of our difficulties—we live in a fallen world and have a vicious adversary—but He doesn't waste our trials. Some of us need that adversity to draw us close to Him and remind us of our dependence on Him because simply hearing His Word is not enough to change us. We have to hear with a heart that knows our own need and is willing to take steps of faith toward Him. When we find ourselves in extreme circumstances, we turn our full attention to God and trust His promises as our lifeline. We choose to believe that He will use the zigzags of our lives for our good and His glory.

Whose purpose and agenda are you most eager to fulfill? There will be moments in your difficult times when all you want is to get through them. You'll probably spend much of your time praying that God will get you out of them. When you understand your purpose—and His purposes for you—you will reach a moment of clarity when you realize that those difficulties are producing something invaluable and eternal in you. You may be going through a hard thing, but I assure you, God is doing a great thing in the midst of it if you'll let Him.

Paul remained focused on his purpose as he was going through his imprisonment and seeing rival preachers take advantage of it to promote themselves. If you've ever been blamed for something that wasn't true, you know how challenging that was for him. A lot of people thought negative things about him because of his situation, and he had plenty of opportunity to dwell on the injustice of it all. Instead, he turned his focus back to his purpose—advancing the gospel and preaching the name of Christ—and rejoiced that the name of Christ was being promoted even by people whose motives weren't entirely selfless. "Whether in pretense or in truth," Jesus was becoming known, and Paul celebrated because making Christ known was his purpose (Phil. 1:18).

Jesus is the prime example of remaining focused on God's purpose regardless of what people think. He often found Himself on the hard side of people's judgments, yet did not allow human opinions to distract Him from His mission. On one occasion, He broke all kinds of cultural norms by talking to a Samaritan woman at a well. If you want a sense of how shocking that was to the disciples, imagine Him having a friendly conversation with someone completely opposite from you in social background, moral behavior, and political views—i.e., the people who offend you most—and think of how you might react. He completely defied the disciples' expectations by talking with this woman while they had gone to get food, and when they asked Him if He wanted something to eat, He told them that He had food they didn't know about: doing the Father's will. That's what it looks like to be rooted in your purpose.

Paul's food was also to do the will of his Father, regardless of what other people were doing or saying, and regardless of the difficult circumstances he was going through. That's your food too, whether you realize it or not. It's very easy in the midst of challenging times to crave an escape, pity yourself as a victim, or be overwhelmed by the pain—which is very real and intense. God never minimizes the heartbreak and suffering you've experienced; however, He does redeem it, accomplishes His purposes through it, and invites you to a higher perspective that leads to joy. If you pause long enough to reflect on what God is doing in your circumstances, you will most likely see ways for the gospel to go forth, other believers to be strengthened, and yourself to be more closely conformed to the image of Christ.

WHEN YOU BECOME GOD'S EXHIBIT A— AND B AND C

You may have noticed that the three purpose statements from this chapter correspond to the three ways God used Paul's circumstances as we discussed them in the last chapter.

- Paul celebrated the gospel going forth through his imprisonment—that it was reaching the lost—and, like him, you are an ambassador and messenger of the gospel.
- Paul recognized that other Christians were bolder because of his example, so his imprisonment was building up the found—and, like him, you are called to encourage God's people and help them grow to maturity in Christ.
- Paul demonstrated depth of character and vision as rival preachers were exploiting his situation. The man was growing deep. And, like him, you are called to serve the living God and become like your Master.

In other words, your circumstances can become occasions to reach the lost, strengthen the church, and make you more like Jesus.

No matter what you're going through, it's a cause for joy. You won't rejoice if you don't see what God is doing and how it connects you with your purpose, but if you do see it—if you understand these core purpose statements and look for how God is fulfilling them through you and in you—you will experience a deep sense of fulfillment. That's worth celebrating.

And that's how recognizing the power of purpose enables you to choose joy.

DISCUSSION/APPLICATION QUESTIONS

1. What in this chapter encouraged you the most and why?

2. How does looking at your challenging circumstances through the lens of purpose transform your perspective?

3. How might God want to use your current circumstances to be a witness to someone in your relational network who doesn't know Jesus?

4. How might God want to use your current circumstances to build up someone in the body of Christ?

5. How might God want to make you more like Jesus in your attitude and character through the challenges or suffering you're going through?

Assignment: Pray the prayer below every morning before you start your day for the next seven days.

"Holy Father, I know You work all things for good and my current circumstances have been either decreed or allowed by You to fulfill Your purposes in my life. Grant me grace today to see how my response might be a testimony to those outside of Christ and/or to a fellow believer. Help me surrender my agenda and my expectations to You today; grant me the grace to have a thankful attitude, knowing your ultimate purpose is to use my current challenges to make me more like Jesus."

CHAPTER 5:

The Power of Hope

Kevin was in his early thirties and in great shape. He had a beautiful family—a loving wife and four kids under twelve. His father-in-law and I were good friends, and that's how I got to know Kevin pretty well.

Kevin felt unusually tired one day and thought he must have worked out too hard the day before, but his wife suggested he go to the doctor to get checked out. After a few tests, Kevin was told he had stage IV lymphoma and about a 12 percent chance of surviving it. The news was so unexpected and devastating, but Kevin was an energetic and resilient guy and entered into treatment with a positive, hopeful attitude.

Theresa and I met with Kevin and his wife before his treatment program. We prayed with them, cried with them, and watched as our church rallied around them. Kevin knew it would be a long journey, but he determined to go through it with faith.

"I'm going to find out what I really believe," Kevin told me. "All my life, I've said I believe in Jesus and an eternity in heaven with

Him. I've raised my kids to trust God's character and believe His promises. I guess this is my chance to see how real my faith is."

Kevin decided to keep a journal on CaringBridge and resolved to be completely honest in it with his thoughts and feelings—no pretense, no embellishments, no effort to make it a good story that people might want to read. He wanted to track his internal journey with Christ in whatever direction it went.

As I read Kevin's journal over the next few months, I was impressed with how brutally honest it was. Some entries were four or five pages written in the middle of the night as he cried out to God with his hopes, fears, doubts, and questions. He deeply believed God, but honestly confessed all the doubts that flooded his mind and the fears that came to the surface whenever he thought about not seeing his children grow up. Like the Old Testament psalmists, he poured his heart out in his written words.

When I went to see Kevin in the hospital, nurses told me they had never seen anything like it—people almost lining up to get to visit him. His attitude and the atmosphere in his room kept drawing people in.

Kevin's battle was long, hard, and often uncertain, but he's healthy now, cancer-free for more than ten years. As we discussed in the last chapter, difficult circumstances can shape us to be more like Jesus; God used Kevin's incredibly difficult experience to do just that and drive him deeper spiritually. Everything he went through taught him lessons he'll never forget. I learned some lessons from his experience too.

LIFE LESSONS

As I look back on some deeply challenging situations of my own and reflect on difficult trials such as Kevin's, I'm reminded of four lessons that have proved most helpful:

Facing Our Mortality Is Both Scary and Clarifying

Every time I read Kevin's journal entries, I was reminded of my own mortality. It kept hitting home that I am going to die. It's really going to happen. When my wife, Theresa, went through cancer treatments a decade earlier, I felt the same way. Every one of us and each of our loved ones is going to die, and that's a frightening thought. It's not nearly as frightening for those of us who believe in Jesus as it is for those who don't know their eternal destiny, but it still brings up a lot of emotions about how short life is on this side of heaven and how we grieve for those who have gone before us. It also causes us to get really clear about what's important and what isn't.

Very Few Things in Life Matter Very Much

When we got the news that Theresa had cancer, we cried together on the couch. I delayed my arrival to a board meeting in California, and when I finally got to the meeting, the board gathered around me with tears and prayers for both of us. There were so many things going on in our lives at that time. I had a book contract I needed to fulfill, a travel schedule, appointments at church, speaking engagements, and many other demands. I walked into the office to talk with my assistant about how to rearrange everything. I asked her to call the publisher to delay the book deadlines—perhaps for a year or two—and to cancel all my speaking engagements for the next year. Then I talked and prayed with the elders, and we came up with a plan: I'd be there for weekend services and a few other responsibilities, but otherwise I needed to be available for my wife. Everything that seemed so important the previous week suddenly seemed almost irrelevant. Things like remodeling the kitchen, my left knee hurting, the pressure of finishing the book, staff hires to be made, how our retirement account was doing . . . all became trivial. It's amazing how we can fill our hearts and minds with things that matter to us when all is well—whether our weekend plans will work out, getting the latest phone upgrade, how our fantasy team is doing—and discover how little those things matter when life is on the line. The wisest man in the world was right when he wrote that there is more wisdom in "the house of mourning" than in "the house of pleasure" (Eccl. 7:4). Some things in life matter very much and some don't matter much at all, and when you face life-threatening situations, the difference becomes crystal clear.

$C + P = E$

I know I'm not introducing a new concept here; you'll recognize that formula from earlier chapters. But in life-or-death situations, the reality of that equation is reinforced like never before. Circumstances plus perception really does equal our experience.

As I read Kevin's journal, I saw a guy who wasn't just fighting against cancer. He was also fighting for an eternal perspective. Again and again, he refused to look at his circumstances through a temporal lens and chose an eternal lens instead.

To illustrate to our church how an eternal perspective works, I had our creative team build a wall next to the pulpit. On one side of the wall were signs and objects that represented the big problems we all face—pressures, anxiety, depression, cancer, financial issues, marital problems, struggles with kids, job loss, and on and on. The other side of the wall had signs and objects that represented Christ—

hope, perfection, eternal life, and everything God promises. I placed the seven-foot wall on the platform so the congregation could view both sides of it. Then I stood behind the wall so that I could only see the problem side of it. The people could see the other side, but from my perspective, I could choose to believe only the problems. Then I got a ladder, opened it up, climbed to the top, and looked over the wall. Nothing on my side of the "problems and pain" wall changed, but my point of view did. I could now see the other side, and that cast everything on my side of the wall in a different light.

That's what an eternal perspective is like. Everybody has issues, but those who focus only on the issues will always feel discouraged and overwhelmed by their struggles. Those who can lift their eyes to see God's purposes and promises beyond the "wall" of this life will live in hope and experience joy. Reading Kevin's journal week after week was a powerful example to me and our entire church. It was raw, it was real, but Kevin kept peering into eternity with a desire for healing and restoration—with the knowledge death would not be the end, that God can and will take care of his family, and Jesus actually knows what's best for him and them; so, let it be so.

> **Finding the "right" circumstances isn't the answer. Getting the right perspective on your circumstances is.**

Unfortunately, many people string themselves along with faint hopes of just getting through their current problems. It's an "if only" perspective: "If I can only get to next year"; "If I can only get that perfect job"; "If only I had more money, a new home, better health, the right mate . . ." But that "if" never comes because every season, every year, every human being comes with unique challenges. You aren't going to experience a problem-free existence on this side of that wall. Finding the "right" circumstances isn't the answer. Getting the right perspective on your circumstances is. Only then can you live in authentic hope.

Only an Eternal Perspective Can Produce Peace and Joy When You're Facing Death

Kevin never tried to sugarcoat anything in his journal. He poured his heart out to the Lord, honestly expressing his desire to be alive, passionately praying for the opportunity to enjoy life, serve God, grow old with his wife, and see his kids grow up. But just as honestly on the other side of those prayers there was also a clear perspective on eternity. He knew Jesus as his Savior, knew he would spend eternity in heaven, and if his journey ended up being a lot shorter than he hoped, he could take comfort in the fact that he would see his wife and kids again one day and enjoy everlasting life together with them.

He was unwavering. "I am going to trust God. I believe there is a heaven, I believe the Bible is true, I believe in God's character, His Spirit lives within me, I have certainty and hope, and I'm going to have an upward focus and an outward focus. And I will use this situation for God's purposes. Those nurses and other patients are going to hear and see Christ, not because of my own strength, but because Christ is in me."[3] Kevin demonstrated the balance every Christian should have. We have a lot of hopes for our time in this world, but above all of those hopes is a deeper, more lasting hope.

Let me pause to ask you some probing but very important questions. How do you choose joy when life is crashing in on you? How do you stay grounded in your purpose when it looks like your purpose on earth might come to an end? How do you live in confidence when you wonder whether you or a loved one will live or die? I'd suggest that the answer is very simple. That's not to say it's easy. It isn't. But it's simple and profound: have an eternal perspective. And that perspective is rooted in one word: hope.

Hope is the oxygen of the soul. You can go without food for several days and water for about three, but if you go without hope for very long, you die. This life is not all there is. If we think it is, we eventually lose hope, but if we anchor our soul in eternity and cling to God's promises, we receive the grace and perseverance to keep going.

So, how do you develop the eternal perspective that gives you the kind of hope that allows you to go through anything without giving up, getting inwardly focused, becoming a victim, or blaming God or others? When life is crashing in and you don't know how things are going to turn out, how can you become the kind of person who makes people wonder: *What do they have that I don't have?*

In other words, when life seems hopeless, how do you live with hope?

A CERTAIN HOPE

We use the word *hope* to mean a lot of things. We hope the weather will be nice this weekend, hope our team wins the big game, hope we get that good job, and hope our kids grow up to be strong believers who make wise choices. But the outcome is not guaranteed in any of those scenarios, is it? When we use *hope* in that sense, we're really talking about desires and wishes. We don't know if things are going to work out, but we "hope" they do.

There's nothing wrong with wishful thinking and "hoping" our desires come to pass, but we need to understand that when the Bible talks about hope, it isn't referring to things that may or may not work out. Biblical hope is a certainty, a guarantee of something yet unseen. When we hope for Christ's return, eternal life in heaven, and the fulfillment of God's promises, we aren't speculating or expressing personal desires. These things are definite and certain. They are on God's eternal timeline; they just haven't happened yet. They are coming, but for now we can only anticipate them. Biblical hope is about looking forward not to possibilities, but to certainties.

> **Biblical hope is a certainty, a guarantee of something yet unseen.**

We can anchor our souls in that kind of hope. Hope based in God's plans and purposes cannot be shaken. Our perspective on that hope might shift back and forth—that's why we need to be intentional about choosing our perspectives—but the foundation of our hope never moves. It is based on God's character and faithfulness.

So, how does this connect with choosing joy? In order to experience a life overflowing with joy, we not only need to understand the power of focus and the power of purpose; but we also need to understand the power of hope. Hope is the third key to experiencing joy regardless of our circumstances. And that key prompts a very significant question about where we've placed our hope.

KEY #3: Hope
QUESTION #3: Where is my hope?

Remember Paul's situation as he writes his letter to the Philippians? He's under house arrest in Rome, unable to continue his itinerant ministry of planting churches and supporting new believers, and awaiting a trial that has been pending for well over two years. How that trial might turn out is still very much up in the air. Paul does not know how it's going to end, but he does know his imprisonment will come to a conclusion one way or another. He will either be released or executed.

Most of us would have huge anxiety issues in that kind of circumstance. It was one of those life-or-death situations we might face after a terminal diagnosis, but also with the stigma of a legal verdict attached to it. Yet in all the uncertainty of his circumstances, with critics and rivals taking advantage of his imprisonment and questioning his status as an apostle, with his life and ministry on the line, he looked ahead at the possibilities in front of him and rejoiced.

Joy in the face of death? That's what an eternal perspective does for us. In fact, Paul is emphatic about it. He has just said he rejoices that Christ is being proclaimed, and as he transitions to the issue of his potential execution, he says it again: "Yes, and I will rejoice" (Phil. 1:18).

Just as he and Silas once sang worship songs in a dark Philippian prison, Paul again rejoices in the face of an ominous situation.

He has been told to go into the world to preach, yet he is confined by chains in Rome; he has been betrayed by friends and subjected to political rivalries in the church, and he faces a trial that could well end with his death. Most people would look at his circumstances and wonder if anything is going right. These are the kinds of setbacks that crush many of us. Yet Paul chooses to rejoice. How could any rational person do that?

He gives us two reasons in verses 19–25, both of which show us how his joy is not based on his circumstances. The first reason is that his deliverance is certain:

> For I know that this will turn out for my deliverance through your prayers and the provision of the Spirit of Jesus Christ, according to my earnest expectation and hope, that I will not be put to shame in anything, but that with all boldness, Christ will even now, as always, be exalted in my body, whether by life or by death. (Phil. 1:19–20)

Paul is completely convinced that he will be delivered. We've seen that when Paul told the Philippians he was praying for their love to increase in real knowledge and discernment (v. 9), he used a word that refers to experiential knowledge. Here he uses a different word when he says, "I know." This one refers to facts—objective realities as reliable as a mathematical equation or a law of physics. He knows for a fact he will be delivered—one way or another.

The word *deliverance* in the New Testament is often the same word translated as "salvation." In fact, the connection between these two English words—deliverance and salvation—is a close one in the Old Testament too. Often when David or another psalmist prayed for salvation, he was talking about deliverance from temporal enemies. When the Red Sea parted, that was a deliverance, or salvation, moment for Israel. Paul is using deliverance in the same way.

REASONS FOR CERTAIN HOPE

I like Paul's run-on sentences. Sometimes he gets going and takes off in several different directions before ending his sentence in a way that may or may not finish off the thought he started with. I can relate. In the long sentence that spans verses 18 through 20, you'll see several phrases added to the main point, but notice this thought threaded through it: "I know that this will turn out for my deliverance . . . according to my earnest expectation and hope, that . . . Christ will, even now, as always, be exalted in my body." Everything between those words is there to explain this primary point. They are very important clauses, but this is the essence of what Paul is saying: He is not focused on his comfort level or safety, but on Christ being exalted.

Why is Paul so certain of his deliverance? He mentions two reasons: the Philippians' prayers and the provision of the Spirit of Jesus (v. 19). Paul didn't see prayer as a shot in the dark or a wish that God might or might not incorporate into His sovereign will. He saw it as a concrete reality, an expression of certain hope. He would agree with James, who wrote, "You do not have because you do not ask" (James 4:2). Both of these apostles were simply echoing the promises of Jesus, who assured His followers that God would answer prayers of faith (Mark 11:24; John 14:13; 15:7). Paul believed that when ordinary people come to God earnestly, get on their knees to intercede for others, and claim His promises by faith, it makes a difference. He knew that if the Philippian Christians were praying in faith for something that would glorify God, it would be done.

> He orchestrates things in a way that honors our prayers and His purposes for His glory.

The second reason for Paul's certainty is the provision of the Spirit. We don't understand exactly how human agency (our prayers) and God's sovereignty (His provision) work together—theologians endlessly debate such things—but they do. God is omniscient and knows all the possibilities in every situation, but He also chooses to partner with human beings as His stewards of His creation, and when we intercede in faith-filled, trusting prayer for God to intervene in our circumstances to accomplish His purposes, He orchestrates things in a way that honors our prayers and His purposes for His glory.

The word for "provision" (*epichoregia*) is loaded with meaning. We get our word *chorus* from it. A wealthy patron in this era felt a certain civic responsibility to fund events and buildings of public interest, and because Greek-style theater was at the center of the arts and social life, that support often went directly to choral dance troupes for theater performances. Patrons rented the amphitheater and covered the expenses for actors, singers, and dancers as benefactors of their city. That's the root behind this word, which suggests ample, abundant, bountiful provision. Paul is saying, in a sense, that the Spirit of Jesus is the "wealthy patron" supporting him through the prayers of these Philippian believers. As they prayed, the Spirit would abundantly provide whatever is needed.

Paul's "earnest expectation"—a phrase Paul seems to have coined himself to refer to his intense, unyielding gaze at the object of his hope—is that he will not be put to shame in anything. His words imply that he is like a runner at the finish line, intensely focused, leaning forward and blocking out every distraction as he focuses on the certainty of God's promise. As far as he is concerned, Christ being glorified in his body is a done deal. God would certainly come through.

It would be easy to assume, as I did when reading this passage as a young believer, that the "deliverance" Paul expected was being freed from imprisonment to continue his ministry throughout the Mediterranean world. But that isn't what he is saying. Remember his purpose? As we saw in the last chapter, he (like all of us) was called to reach the lost, build up the found, and grow deep in becoming like Jesus. He still doesn't know if he is going to be released or executed—he makes that clear in the next few verses.

All he knows is that Jesus is going to be exalted in his body, whether through life or death.

So, he isn't focused on being delivered from his imprisonment. He's focused on being delivered from the possibility of compromising his commitment, being unfaithful in his testimony, and falling short of his calling to glorify Jesus. Paul is determined not to fail this assignment. He earnestly expects to remain faithful to the end, thanks to the prayers of the Philippian church and the power of the Holy Spirit; whenever the end happens to come.

Let that sink in. As much as we love Jesus and want to serve Him well, in that circumstance you and I might be focused on life-or-death issues—specifically how much longer we had to live. Paul's main concern was not his freedom or even his possible death. It was Jesus' reputation.

I began this chapter with Kevin's story because at the point in my ministry when he was going through his treatment, I had never met someone with that level of conviction about the reality of heaven and God's promises. Like Paul, Kevin knew that whatever God says about eternity or anything else, you can bank on it.

Paul counted on it to the point that whether he lived or died was secondary to whether or not Jesus was glorified in his life. He might live for Jesus' glory or die for Jesus' glory, but as long as glorifying Jesus was the end result, he was content. In fact, as we'll see in the next chapter, he saw pros and cons to each possibility and didn't know which one he preferred. But he knew he could trust that God knew what was best for him and most fruitful for God's kingdom.

HOW DOES GOD DELIVER US?

It should be clear that Paul defined "deliverance" much differently than we do, which raises the question of what we can expect and believe when we find ourselves in difficult or painful circumstances. On one hand, we don't want to assume that God always comes to the rescue in the ways we'd like Him to rescue us. On the other hand, we don't want to go to the other extreme and assume that God walks with us through our difficulties but never helps us out of them. Scripture gives us plenty of examples of His deliverance, and it takes a variety of forms. Sometimes it's exactly what His people were hoping for.

That's the kind of deliverance we usually think of, but Scripture actually shows us three ways God delivers us. We might call them plan A, plan B, and plan C. That's not how God thinks of them, obviously; He knows up front which plan is best for us. But we do have our preferences and often pray for our idea of plan A—a miraculous deliverance.

God Delivers Us Out of Something

From a human perspective, this is the most dramatic kind of deliverance. We want to be removed from our circumstances— or have them removed from us—and God does it for us. This is what happened in Acts 12 when Peter was in prison and the whole church was praying for him. An angel woke Peter up, the chains fell off his wrists, and Peter was able to walk out of the prison into his freedom. Even the people praying for him had a hard time believing he had been set free. God miraculously delivered him out of a threatening situation.

There were times early in our ministry when Theresa and I had no money and couldn't pay the rent or buy groceries, and somehow God would meet our needs in a way that seemed miraculous to us. Once we got an unexpected check in the mail from a guy I had met years earlier when he was in high school. He had since become a professional quarterback, and his surprise gift paid for our rent and groceries for a month. One time we got a letter and a check from a missionary in India on the same day our bills were due. There have been times when we have anointed people with oil, prayed for them, and seen a brain tumor miraculously go—not from any special gift of healing, but because that's how God wanted to do it. I've prayed for other people the same way and preached at their funeral soon afterward. I don't understand why He sometimes delivers that way and sometimes doesn't, but I know He still does miracles.

That's one way He delivers, and we have plenty of stories from the Bible and from today's experiences to prove it. That doesn't mean we don't have enough faith if He chooses another way. Some people say it's all a matter of believing strongly and consistently enough and speaking it out loud by faith, while others go in the opposite direction and fatalistically assume our prayers aren't going to change anything. Somewhere in between those extremes, God works on our behalf in response to our prayers of faith, and sometimes He intervenes with a miracle or some unusual, unexpected provision to deliver us out of the adversity or difficulty.

I confess that even after being a Christian for more than fifty years, I always pray for plan A, "Please Lord, do a supernatural miracle and deliver me, or someone I love, out of this situation." And yet, after walking with the Lord many years, I can look back and recognize God's wisdom when He had a different plan. Not one I would choose for myself, or for others, but one that accomplished something far deeper and more lasting than simply solving a temporary problem, or healing a sickness, or providing money just in the nick of time. That's what we will look at next.

God Delivers Us Through Something

This is what Paul experienced in 2 Corinthians 12. He had had amazing experiences receiving revelation from God and was given a "thorn" in his flesh to keep him from getting proud. We don't know what that thorn was—speculation ranges from some kind of physical illness or infirmity to human critics or enemies, which is how a "thorn in the side" is used in the Old Testament (Num. 33:55; Judg. 2:3; Ezek. 28:24). Whatever it was, Paul prayed three times that God would deliver him from it.

Paul had pretty strong faith and a track record of miracles. You'd think his prayers would be answered, right? Well, they were, but not with the kind of deliverance he was asking for. His prayer was that the thorn, whatever it was, would leave him. But that isn't how God answered. God told him instead, "My grace is sufficient for you, for power is perfected in weakness." Paul therefore gladly chose to embrace his weaknesses as opportunities to experience the power of Christ (2 Cor. 12:8–10). In other words, "I'll leave the circumstances in place, but give you what you need in the midst of them." God delivered Paul, but not by taking the circumstances away. He delivered Paul *through* the circumstances, not *from* them.

God uses these kinds of opportunities to refine us and strengthen our faith and character. This is where we discover that even in the midst of difficult situations, He can give us unexplainable peace, joy, and contentment. In fact, this is what Paul got out of his adversity; he leaned into that one and many others—insults, distresses, persecutions, and difficulties (2 Cor. 12:10)—with rejoicing. He found that in whatever ways he was weak, that was where he would find God's strength. His problems gave God an opportunity to show up in power.

You can't have that perspective if you believe life is short and you have to get the most enjoyment out of it while you can. But if you have an eternal perspective, anything you go through during the course of your life can have much larger, everlasting implications. For example, let's imagine you walk outside, and you see a green wire suspended in the air about six feet off the ground going as far as you can see to the east, and as far as you can see to the west. This small, green wire extends forever and ever in both directions. Let's assume that wire or line represents eternity. I want you to picture a small piece of paper, one inch long and one-half inch wide, attached to the green line right in front of your face. Let's imagine that one inch rep-

> That tiny, tiny little dot on that one inch of paper called time represents your entire life.

resents all of time since the very beginning. Now, I want you to get out a magnifying glass and move it very close to the piece of paper and on it you can see a very, very small little dot. So microscopic that it's hard to see with the naked eye. That tiny, tiny little dot on that one inch of paper called time represents your entire life. If you learn to see this earthly life as a tiny speck on that endless string, you might begin to care a lot more about eternal issues on the vast length of the line outside the dot than the momentary pleasures and comforts within it. Perspective is powerful.

In his book *Mere Christianity*, C. S. Lewis alludes to a dot and line concept in which there are two kinds of believers: those who live for the dot and those who live for the line. The dot is very important. It has an effect on our eternity. But when pain or difficulty comes, we need to remember its purpose. We need to be able to look beyond the dot and into the line.

This is why we read the Bible, pray, fast, and practice spiritual disciplines. It's all meant to redirect our focus to what really matters and live in the hope that spans the length of that line. The reason I spend time in the morning talking with my heavenly Father while I read His Word and have my coffee, is that I know the world will bombard me all day long with a very temporal mindset. The only way I can get an eternal mindset is to tap into the mind of Christ and the Spirit who lives in me. The reason I hang out with people who have a lot of faith is that their faith is contagious. I want to catch it and see with eyes that are focused on eternity.

Not everything works out the way we want it to. God has a bigger agenda than we do.

We don't get brownie points for any of our spiritual practices. Measuring up to some divine standard isn't the point. The main purpose is to connect us relationally with the God who transforms us and gives us the revelation and vision to "see" the unseen reality beyond our visible circumstances.

Not everything works out the way we want it to. God has a bigger agenda than we do. He wants to make us more and more like Jesus. I wish there was an easier way, but suffering seems to be one of the major ways He shapes our heart and character. Peter wrote about how suffering reorients us from sin to living for the will of God (1 Peter 4:1–2). By God's design in this fallen world, He uses evil and suffering to draw us nearer to Himself. It's good to seek Him even when all is going well for us, and many people do. But more often, I've seen people who had little regard for God suddenly begin pouring their hearts out in prayer when their lives fall apart or a loved one is dying. They stop living for the dot and begin living for the line.

That often doesn't happen when God delivers us "out of" our circumstances, but it does when He delivers us "through them."

God Delivers Us unto Himself

Some other pastors and I were talking recently about how people today view life and death, and we agreed on how odd it is that most Christians think the worst thing that can happen to a person is to die. We can understand how people who don't believe in Jesus or eternity might think so, but for those of us who have been promised a blissful eternity with Him? That seems like a strange perspective. It certainly wasn't the perspective of Paul. He rejoiced that Christ would be exalted whether he lived or died—and wrote that dying and being with Christ would be even better.

Both of my parents died of long, debilitating, painful diseases. By the time they died, I was grateful—not that they were gone, but that they were no longer in pain. Watching them live through that experience was difficult, which is why I think the psalmist wrote, "Precious in the sight of the LORD is the death of His godly ones" (Ps. 116:15). If you believe we only have the temporal—that life is all about our time in this world—then death is dreadful. You end up with nothing. But, if you believe there really is a heaven and God's promises are all true, you know it's better to depart and be with Christ. That sustains you and fills you with hope.

Paul wrote that if there is no resurrection, if we've hoped for Christ in this life only, we should be pitied above everyone else (1 Cor. 15:19). But because the resurrection is a certain hope, there's no reason for us to cling to everything in this life as though it's all we have. That doesn't mean we should live with an escapist, pie-in-the-sky mentality. Suffering is real, and sometimes life is incredibly painful. There's no getting around that. But we are called to set our minds on things above, not on things on earth (Col. 3:2), and live with a clear view of eternity, even in the midst of our darkest, most excruciating experiences. Like Paul, we need to understand that to live is Christ and to die is gain (Phil. 1:21)—and, with eager expectation, fix our eyes on the promised hope.

EVERY DELIVERANCE IS A CAUSE FOR JOY

If you've been a Christian for very long, you can probably recall times when God delivered you from something and other times when He delivered you through something. You may be asking God for deliverance right now and wondering why plan A isn't happening. If so, be encouraged. He is not ignoring your pleas for deliverance; He may instead be drawing you closer, transforming your character, and reorienting your perspective while He delivers you through your circumstances.

If you've lost someone close to you and wondered why God didn't deliver your loved one from death, understand that sometimes He delivers His people from life in this world into their eternal home to be with Him. It's our human tendency to draw conclusions based on the "dot" of our earthly lives, but God always urges us to lift our eyes toward the infinite line of eternity. In one way or another, He always delivers His people.

That's why Paul had joy in the midst of what appeared to be horrendous circumstances. He knew his deliverance was certain. He counted on God's faithfulness and eagerly expected that Christ would be glorified in him, whether in his life or his death. And if death came, Paul knew he would be immediately ushered into the presence of Christ.

That's a certain hope—and always a reason for joy.

DISCUSSION/APPLICATION QUESTIONS

1. What's one thing from this chapter that you want to remember going forward? Why?

2. What's the difference between how we often use the word *hope* and its meaning in Scripture?

3. How did Paul's eternal perspective shape his evaluation of his life-or-death circumstances?

4. When has God delivered you "out of" a challenging circumstance or delivered you "through" one?

5. How does asking the question "Where is my hope?" force you to think differently about your difficult circumstance?

Assignment: Although God at times miraculously delivers us out of suffering and pain, more often He delivers us through it. Write down on an index card the verse below, and ask God to help you experience His power in your weakness as the apostle Paul did.

And He has said to me, "My grace is sufficient for you, for power is perfected in weakness." Most gladly, therefore, I will rather boast about my weaknesses, so that the power of Christ may dwell in me. Therefore I am well content with weaknesses, with insults, with distresses, with persecutions, with difficulties, for Christ's sake; for when I am weak, then I am strong.
(2 Cor. 12:9–10)

CHAPTER 6:

How to Experience Unshakable Hope

I love to share stories of people like Kevin who put their full hope in Christ amid life's most difficult challenges. As a pastor for more than thirty-five years, I've been very up close and personal with many who face life-and-death issues. Regardless of what we say or think we believe, a diagnosis with life-threatening outcomes has a way of clarifying in what or whom we have put our hope. It was true of the apostle Paul and it's true of all of us.

Kevin's story reminds me that the same grace that the apostle Paul was given is available to ordinary people like you and me as well. Unfortunately, decades of pastoring have also allowed me a very personal and at times painful perspective of many who put their hope elsewhere.

I will never forget, as a young pastor, the tragic experience of a middle-aged woman who was diagnosed with cancer. She had started reading books and attending meetings that taught her if she believed "hard enough" that God guaranteed she would be healed.

The real test of that belief was refusing any medical treatment. She had a husband who was not a follower of Christ, and a very tender and impressionable daughter who attended our youth group and was deeply concerned about her mom.

The mom had been a strong and active Christian in our church. I met with her on several occasions to encourage her to examine her new beliefs in light of Scripture and to get the medical help that she needed. I also later intervened when she became more and more ill, in hopes that she would begin to prepare her husband and daughter for what looked to be the inevitable.

The mother refused to discuss her possible death or deal with any of the issues that she was going through because in her mind, "that was not exercising faith." She had been taught to never say out loud anything negative and to constantly "believe" that she would be healed, because God had promised it, if she just believed hard and well enough. The result was a dying woman telling her family and everyone who would listen that she was already healed and was simply "claiming it."

It's certainly true that God chooses to supernaturally heal in our day. I've had the privilege of witnessing that on several occasions. But she was putting her hope not in God, but in her faith, and in a false belief that God will heal everyone all the time, if they simply "believe hard enough."

The mother died without ever having any closure with her daughter or her husband. She had prayed for her husband's salvation for many years. Yet her false hope communicated to her husband that God doesn't hear, and God doesn't answer prayers. He was not interested in exploring a relationship with Christ after her death and her daughter left the church because God did not answer her mother's prayer. Who can believe in a God like that?

Sometimes we mistakenly think as believers in Jesus that putting our hope in other things is always something secular like money, fame, career, or gaining the approval of others; but sometimes our false beliefs about God can be idols as well. We put our hope in our own righteousness, our own spiritual disciplines, our church attendance, our moral superiority, or our generosity—all with a view that "God owes me a good life and things will go my way."

Many people are disappointed with God because their hopes did not work out like they thought. Maybe they misunderstood God's promises or unconsciously thought that if they did all the right things—served God faithfully, gave generously, and prayed often—that He would spare them from hardship and pain. Even when we know better than that, we still buy into some of these implicit assumptions about how life with God works. And it's true that He is extremely generous, gracious, and kind. He does bless us. But He never guarantees that we won't suffer.

That's why He asks us to put our hope in Him, not in circumstances. If we live with an expectation that He will make everything work out the way we want, we will be shaken when they don't. But if we are rooted and grounded in our source of joy—God Himself—we cannot be moved. Circumstances are powerless to rob our joy if our source of joy is an eternal, unchanging, unshakable hope.

TO LIVE IS CHRIST . . .

Reason number one that Paul lived with hope in the midst of his circumstances was that he was certain of his deliverance—not the removal of his circumstances, necessarily, but his deliverance through them. He was confident that he would not be put to shame, that he would maintain his testimony without compromise, and that Christ would be glorified through him, whether he lived or *died.* For Paul, that was a huge reason to rejoice.

There's another reason, too, as Paul tells us in the next few verses. He has this hope because the source of his joy is unshakable. Our circumstances may get better or worse, incomes rise or fall, storms come and go, relationships sail along smoothly or hit rough patches, kids make you proud or do disappointing things, health remains strong or suddenly fails . . . virtually every area of life has its ups and downs. You can live like a cork on the waves of circumstances, bobbing around wherever life takes you, or you can anchor yourself in eager expectation of the certain hope God has given you.

> You can live like a cork on the waves of circumstances, bobbing around wherever life takes you, or you can anchor yourself in eager expectation of the certain hope God has given you.

As we've seen, joy doesn't just happen to us. It's a choice.

Even in imprisonment and the possibility of death, Paul knew that the source of his joy was unshakable. He anchored his soul in heaven, confident that God's promises would sustain him and Jesus would be glorified in him.

Here's how he explains his perspective on life and death:

For to me, to live is Christ and to die is gain. But if I am to live on in the flesh, this will mean fruitful labor for me; and I do not know which to choose. But I am hard-pressed from both directions, having the desire to depart and be with Christ, for that is very much better; yet to remain on in the flesh is more necessary for your sake. Convinced of this, I know that I will remain and continue with you all for your progress and joy in the faith, so that your proud confidence in me may abound in Christ Jesus through my coming to you again. (Phil. 1:21–26)

"To live is Christ." In other words, while we are in the flesh, with the Spirit of Jesus at work within us, we are representatives and ambassadors of Christ on earth. But "to die is gain." Going to live with Jesus face-to-face in heaven is obviously a better situation for us.

Paul recognizes the pros and cons of each side of that dichotomy. On one hand, Christ living through him on earth means more fruitfulness. We will never have an opportunity to bear eternal fruit in this world after we've gone to heaven. This is it—our only shot at planting seeds on earth that result in a harvest that lasts forever. On the other hand, our ultimate goal is eternal life with Jesus, the end of all suffering and pain. We will not be talking about adversity or difficult circumstances in heaven.

Paul juxtaposes those two realities and ends up saying, in essence, "I don't know! I'm torn! What am I going to do?"

But Paul knows what is best for the Philippians and the other churches he has started: "to remain on in the flesh." He knows his time of death will come, whether sooner or later. But if he's choosing—and he seems to suggest in verse 22 that he might have a choice in the matter—he would leverage his platform in this temporal world to bear eternal fruitfulness just a little bit longer.

TO DIE IS GAIN

This idea that "to die is gain" seems foreign to many modern American Christians. Believers in other countries live with that perspective because they have experienced persecution and are not swept up in a materialist culture that majors on a "you only live once" mentality. Many of us cannot relate to that, but we need to immerse ourselves not in what our culture tells us about life and death, but what the Bible says.

According to Paul, our outer selves are decaying while our inner selves are being renewed daily, so we do not lose heart. In fact, our "light affliction is producing for us an eternal weight of glory far beyond all comparison," and we therefore focus on what is unseen rather than what is seen (2 Cor. 4:16–18). That's the foundation of our unshakable hope and joy. We can rejoice because an eternal weight of glory awaits us—even when our bodies are wasting away.

I have had the privilege of witnessing the joy and hope of two people even as their bodies waste away. The first is Joni Eareckson Tada. You may be familiar with her story. She was injured at age seventeen in a diving accident and became a quadriplegic, and since then has written multiple books, spoken globally, and founded Joni and Friends, a ministry providing wheelchairs and resources to disabled people around the world. I'd certainly heard of her and even watched a few videos, but had never met her personally.

> **Without any pretense or sounding "overly spiritual," she told me how deeply she longed to be with Jesus and have a new body.**

A number of years ago, I was speaking at an event in which Joni was also speaking. They have what's called a "green room" where you wait for your turn to speak and have a little time to meet with the other speakers. It just so happened that we were the only two in the room, and we had a conversation that I doubt she even remembers; but it had a profound impact in my life.

She shared honestly what a struggle it was each and every day to do the most mundane of things: have someone comb her hair, roll her over, put on her makeup, and help her get into her wheelchair. Without any pretense or sounding "overly spiritual," she told me how deeply she longed to be with Jesus and have a new body. She talked openly about fighting depression and the temptation toward self-pity, and then began to share about the intimacy with Jesus that has sustained her. I don't want to exaggerate, but there was almost a visible "glow" as she shared about her intimate relationship with Jesus, and His sustaining grace. She modeled a yearning and a desire to be with Him in heaven like what the apostle Paul described.

The second person is a man named John Paine. I met him once personally in Dallas and then later, in a very unexpected way. His story is told in the book *The Luckiest Man*. (I highly recommend it, especially for anyone going through what feels like an unfair, devastating life experience, and wondering where God is in it all.)

I won't spoil the book, but the short version is that it is about an incredibly successful businessman in the Dallas area who had everything life could offer. A beautiful wife and family, wealth, influence, a leadership role in the church, and an authentic relationship with Jesus admired by many. Then came ALS (Lou Gehrig's disease), which progressively took over his life, his body, and his speech, and confined him to a wheelchair with blinking out one letter at a time being his only means of communication.

John sent me the manuscript of his book and asked if I would consider endorsing it. My life was packed and busy and I didn't know him that well, so I intended to quickly scan it to see if I could say something positive. But I was hooked within the first few pages, and found myself opening it every spare minute that I could squeeze into my schedule. John was describing the kind of relationship that I had tasted and longed for, but in a way well beyond anything I had ever experienced. His

> **The answer to your problem is not a solution. It's a person.**

hope, his joy, and his attitude in circumstances one hundred times more difficult than mine both humbled and inspired me.

Most of us spend quite a bit of effort trying to avoid our troubles. We don't want to waste away, so we postpone our mortality as long as possible. There's no shame in that; it's a human response. But we forget that the "worst" that can happen to us—death—leads to an eternal weight of glory. We get to rejoice with Jesus forever.

Someone once told me in the midst of a very difficult situation, "The answer to your problem is not a solution. It's a person." That's so true. I want to fix everything. It's human nature. But before solutions and fixes, there's a more important response. "Jesus, I need to see this Your way. I need Your strength." Getting us out of our situation isn't always the answer. But He is always the answer in the midst of it. We need to act like we really believe He's alive and demonstrating His presence and power in our lives.

Paul doesn't question the presence and power of Jesus in his life, so he is "convinced of this": that he will remain with the Philippians—that is, on earth—for their "progress and joy in the faith" (Phil. 1:25). Coming to them again once he is released will vindicate their confidence in him and increase their faith in Jesus (v. 26). This is the conclusion he comes to even as he is writing the letter and the Spirit of God is speaking to him.

Unlike a lot of people who have been raised in Western evangelicalism, Paul understands that the goal of life is to know, love, enjoy, and serve God and share Him with as many people as possible while we are on earth. The most important thing is not to go to the right school, make the right amount of money, and fulfill all your personal goals while also being a Christian. It's to glorify Jesus by reflecting His heart and nature, even if glorifying Him requires the ultimate sacrifice. He is not an add-on to our lives. All of life revolves around Him.

Everything in life goes around something. You can see this even through a microscope or a telescope. Electrons revolve around the nucleus of an atom, and planets revolve around a star. Our lives as human beings revolve around whatever we've chosen as our center. For many people, that's an agenda, an ambition, another person, or some defining anchor point. But we're designed to revolve around God, and anything else throws our life out of sync with His purposes. That's why so many people wrestle with a sense of meaninglessness or futility and wonder what life is all about. They are revolving around some unworthy center that will ultimately prove to be pointless.

Paul tells the Philippians essentially that his life orbits around Jesus. It's all for Him. If he lives, it's fruitfulness for Jesus, and if he dies, it's face-to-face fellowship with Jesus. Both of those are appealing options, and he's torn between the two. It's a win-win situation.

Christianity was never just a religion for Paul. It wasn't about following certain precepts to live a good life or adhering to a moral code. He didn't approach it as something he needed for himself in order to be fulfilled (though it was certainly fulfilling). Believing in Jesus was a life-transforming relationship of deep connection with God. The Spirit of God lived within him, just as He does with us, and Paul anchored himself in that reality and cultivated that relationship like few have ever done. As he writes later in this letter (3:8), there is nothing more valuable than knowing Jesus.

Can you see how that stirs up an excitement and anticipation for living with Jesus in a face-to-face relationship with no barriers? Paul had a brief encounter with Jesus on the Damascus road (Acts 9:1–9) and had fellowshipped with Jesus in the Spirit ever since. He experienced God's presence and received deep revelation. But that wasn't the end goal. He was still living in the flesh—by now, flesh that was tired and sore from years of violent attacks—and seeing God and eternal realities only partially, as if through a dirty glass or dimmed mirror (1 Cor. 13:12). Every day for him was one day closer to seeing Jesus in full view.

At the same time, the Philippians and many other churches could still use some good teaching. They still had problems that needed to be resolved and questions that needed to be answered. Paul's plan A was to be delivered out of his circumstances—out of his life in the flesh and into open fellowship with Jesus—but he understood the wisdom of plan B, being delivered through his circumstances and continuing to help believers in this world. That's the side he comes down on in verses 25–26. He'll stay on earth as long as God wants him to stay.

PAUL'S SECRET

When Paul wrote his second letter to the Corinthians, probably about five or six years before he wrote to the Philippians, he had been brutally whipped five times, beaten with rods three times, stoned once, shipwrecked three times, and in dangerous situations from rivers, robbers, Jews, gentiles, and travels through wilderness and seas. He had labored hard, hungered and thirsted, gone without sleep, and endured harsh conditions. And he had been through all of this while handling the daily pressure of building and supporting churches that were nearly constantly threatened by external opposition and internal divisions (2 Cor. 11:24–28).

> Paul did not learn the keys to joy and hope in a vacuum. He discovered them in the fires of affliction.

He wrote about being "afflicted in every way, but not crushed; perplexed, but not despairing; persecuted, but not forsaken; struck down, but not destroyed; always carrying about in the body the dying of Jesus, so that the life of Jesus also may be manifested in our body" (2 Cor. 4:8–10). It's not much of a stretch to believe he was clinically depressed at times, nearly at the end of his rope, while still maintaining his focus on ultimate reality.

Paul did not learn the keys to joy and hope in a vacuum. He discovered them in the fires of affliction.

What was his secret? How, in the context of all those hardships and frustrations, did he tap into the unshakable source of his hope and joy? As his words in Philippians 1 have shown us again and again, he chose the right perspective—or, as we might call it, a strategic vantage point.

I looked up definitions of a "vantage point" and love how it's described. It's a position or situation more advantageous than the opponent's, which certainly applies to Paul's perspective. But another definition is even more relevant: it's a position that allows a clear, broad view or understanding.[4]

> **With the right vantage point, we see the things that are unseen.**

The question we need to ask is not just, *Where is my hope?* Take it a step further: *From what vantage point am I looking for my hope?*

Paul was looking at life from the right position. In that passage where he talked about being "afflicted in every way" and dying the death of Jesus in order to exhibit the life of Jesus, he went on to explain why "we do not lose heart." It's the same reason he believed that "to die is gain"—that an eternal weight of glory is being produced by our momentary afflictions (2 Cor. 4:16–17). Because of that, "we look not at the things which are seen, but at the things which are not seen; for the things which are seen are temporal, but the things which are not seen are eternal" (2 Cor. 4:18).

Did you notice the visual words in that last verse—Paul's vantage point? It's all about what we "look at" and "see." With the right vantage point, we see the things that are unseen. Our natural eyes see what is temporal, but eyes of faith see what is eternal.

A great story in 2 Kings illustrates "seeing the unseen" dramatically. The prophet Elisha's camp was surrounded by enemy forces, and Elisha's servant was panicking. Elisha simply told him not to be afraid—that there were more for them than against them—and then prayed that God would open the servant's eyes. Suddenly the servant was able to see all of God's invisible forces on the mountain, and they far outnumbered the enemy (2 Kings 6:15–17). The spiritual world was just as real—and much more encouraging—than the physical world around them.

If our vantage point relies on our natural vision, we will likely lose hope and miss out on joy whenever life gets difficult. But if our vantage point is like Paul's—a vision of unseen realities based on the revelation God has given us in Scripture—even our most challenging circumstances can be lined with hope.

If you think that last line might be a bit of an exaggeration, let me share a letter that I received from a prisoner on death row a number of years ago:

I am a sinner, condemned by man, and saved by Christ.

My journey to find my way to Christ was long in coming, including 5+ years in the county jail awaiting trial, followed by 4+ years on San Quentin's death row. However, once God turned my heart to Him, I soon realized my journey has just begun to follow Christ.

It is this journey, following Christ, and all that that entails that makes God's use of you to help me so very much.

I used to spend my days here on the death row going outside and buffing out my body; 4-1/2 years of that brought nothing but a muscular body. A muscular body that will fade and die. So, really nothing came of all that time and effort. Indeed, only bad came from it, as I had also immersed myself in the heat and discontent this place nurtures and feeds off of.

A Napa Christian, who occasionally attends your services, was blessed with the patience and persistence that finally brought me through my gestation period of my spiritual birth, as well as directing me to hear your program on KFAX Radio.

Now I have shed myself of my old ways, I stay in my cell, do my artwork and listen to the weekday morning broadcast. However, when 11 AM rolls around, I push everything aside and break out my Bible and not just listen, but I study along with you. I look forward to hearing you each and every weekday.

I want to thank you Pastor Ingram for your service to God and taking me through the Bible the way you do so I can really understand it and apply it to my life.

I'm still on death row, but now, with God's Word dwelling within me and growing daily, I am happier than I've ever been in my life. I thank God every day for coming into my heart, and count myself so very blessed to be His humble servant, and spreading His Word with the wonderful help of your service in the name of Christ.

Thank you again Pastor Ingram to you and to your staff. I wish you all a blessed new year.

Trusting in Christ,

(Name withheld)

As strange as it seems, for those who are honest, the prospect of death brings amazing clarity about where our hope resides. The prisoner's letter reminds me of Christians I've met returning to countries where certain death will be their future if they continue sharing their faith, and so they have an awareness of God's presence and power like few others. Their testimonies have been a great encouragement for me to ask myself, "Where am I putting my hope?"

WHERE IS YOUR HOPE?

What gets you discouraged? When you're frustrated, angry, disappointed, what's underneath those feelings? Have you placed your hope in upward mobility, a perfect marriage, perfect kids, or perfect health? Of course, it isn't wrong to hope for a good income, family life, and health. But if you anchor your hope in these things—if your life orbits around them as though your joy depends on them—you're setting yourself up for discouragement.

The underlying question beneath all the others is this: Can you say that to live is Christ and to die is gain?

Everyone wants life to go well and to be successful—however they define success, which is often in terms of health, income (and the possessions and experiences it can buy), and relationships. It would be wrong to conclude that success, money, health, and fulfilling relationships are bad; but they make very bad and capricious gods.

So, what does your life really revolve around? I'm not asking what it *should* revolve around. You know the right answer to that. But if you look at the evidence in your financial statements and calendars—where you invest your money and time—what does it tell you about your priorities? Are they eternal? What do you and your family and friends talk about most passionately? What dreams and desires are on your mind when you wake up in the morning and lie down at night? Please don't hear a harsh or demanding tone in my words. Yes, they are direct and perhaps very challenging; but if your hope is not in Christ, your life and your dreams are headed for disaster.

The underlying question beneath all the others is this: Can you say that to live is Christ and to die is gain? You may go to church, sing praises to God, pray every day, and try to be a good, God-honoring person, but that still doesn't answer the question. I've known people—myself included—who do all of that and still orient their lives around another person, a job, or a strong desire or ambition. We all do it. But God calls all of us every day to keep reorienting ourselves around Him—because to do otherwise is to make that goal, activity, or person an idol. God and God alone is worthy of our highest affection, and He loves us and wants us to experience His "good and acceptable, and perfect will" for our lives (Rom. 12:2).

This calling is true all the time, but it especially hits home when our false sources of hope are threatened—when you've lost a career or a spouse or been given a few months to live. In times like that, you really need to know what's on the other side of the wall between time and eternity. You need a vantage point where you can look over that wall and see the eternal weight of glory behind it. When you have that vision, you can live through anything today with an unshakable source of joy and hope.

Remember, when life is crashing in on you, you have a choice. I encourage you to give up control of your life to an all-knowing, all-powerful, good and loving God who sent His Son to die in your place and rise from the dead. In exchange, you are united to Him and given an entirely new life that is eternal and filled with purpose, hope, and joy. If any idols have crept in—if your life revolves around anything other than Him—simply repent of those false hopes and anchor yourself in the unshakable source of true hope.

Don't breeze past that last sentence. It is so easy when we read a book to intellectually acknowledge, "Wow! I need to address that" and then just keep reading as though somehow being aware of and acknowledging an idol in our life changes something. Pause, right now, and ponder that question honestly before God: "Have any idols crept into my life? Does my life revolve around something or someone other than Jesus?" If so, admit it. Come to Him right now and own up to that reality. Ask God to forgive you, cleanse you, and give you the will and wisdom to make whatever changes are necessary. Finally, go public with someone today. Tell them, text them, call them, or Zoom them and share what's going on in your life and ask for their prayer and help. Real repentance will require more than confession. None of us make major changes without God's power *and* the help and support of godly brothers and sisters.

Like Paul, you will be able to look at your life—and even its biggest life-or-death issues—and know that to live is Christ and to die is gain. From that vantage point, even your most challenging circumstances can be filled with hope. Like Paul, we can set our face like flint and know with certainty that in His goodness and wisdom, He will deliver us—either "out of" or "through" or "unto Himself." He will never leave or forsake us. We are His children!

DISCUSSION/APPLICATION QUESTIONS

1. What story in this chapter grabbed your attention the most and why?

2. Where are you tempted to put your hope apart from Christ? Family? Work? Success? Your looks or intellect? Your religious service? Other?

3. Read 1 John 5:11–13. What does this passage teach about having full assurance of eternal life? Who can know for sure they have eternal life? How sure are you?

4. What specific step of faith/obedience do you sense that the Holy Spirit is prompting you to take as it relates to putting your hope fully in Christ and not anything or anyone else?

5. The prosperity gospel promises believers that if they love God and do what He commands, they can expect financial blessing, healing, and a trouble-free life. How can this lead to being disillusioned with God?

Assignment: When we suffer and experience pain and injustice, we're often tempted to question God's love for us. Write the verse below on an index card and place it where you'll see it multiple times this week. Read it out loud slowly and thank God that it is true.

> For I am convinced that neither death, nor life, nor angels, nor principalities, nor things present, nor things to come, nor powers, nor height, nor depth, nor any other created thing, will be able to separate us from the love of God, which is in Christ Jesus our Lord. (Romans 8:38–39)

CHAPTER 7:

The Power of Expectations

Fred and Bebe are wonderful friends who had become like an uncle and aunt to our children. They are practically family. So much so that they sat with us at all of our children's weddings. When we heard that Bebe had gone in for some tests and found out she had colon cancer, it was devastating.

When Bebe's surgery was scheduled, she was told that the doctors would take about twelve inches out of her colon and she would have to stay in the hospital for six days. Afterward, at least for a time if not permanently, she would need to wear a bag on her side and require follow-up surgery at some point in the future.

We prayed leading up to the surgery and while Bebe was going through it. After the surgery, I went to the hospital to see how she was doing. I was going not as a pastor, but as a friend heartbroken by this tragic turn of events. When I walked into her hospital room, Bebe was glowing.

"How are you doing?" I asked.

"Great!" she said.

"Really? What happened?"

"They were planning to take out twelve inches, but they only took four. I'm not going to need a bag strapped to my side, and probably won't need any more surgeries. Instead of being in here six days, like they told me, I'll be out tomorrow. I'm so encouraged! And so very thankful to God!"

Now, with Bebe's experience in mind, I want you to picture another woman who was brought to the same hospital for a biopsy; let's call her Gladys.

"We're going to do a little exploratory surgery," the doctor told Gladys. "But I've been a doctor for years, and I've seen this many times before. It's probably benign. We just need to go in, check it out, and make sure. You'll probably be out of here sometime tomorrow."

When I go in to see Gladys the next day, I ask her how everything went.

"I just can't believe it. They took four inches out of my colon, and I'm going to be here six days. I've got cancer!"

What's the difference between those two scenes? Expectations. One lady went in expecting something terrible and was thrilled when it turned out to be much less. The other went in expecting nothing serious and was devastated when it turned out to be more. Yet their outcomes were exactly the same.

Here's another example—completely hypothetical, but it drives home the point. Imagine a couple who goes out to dinner for their anniversary, leaving their three kids at home. One of their children is old enough to babysit the other two, so the children are home alone while this couple enjoys their anniversary date. But halfway through dinner, the couple gets an urgent phone call. A neighbor tells them their house is on fire.

"The firefighters have come, and we're searching for the kids but haven't found them yet," the neighbor says frantically. "Please get home as soon as you can."

The couple gets in the car, drives home as fast as they can, screaming and crying on the way, desperately hoping their kids are okay. When they arrive, they see the firefighters trying to put out the blazing fire that has almost gutted their home. They run around knocking on neighbors' doors, looking between houses and in bushes, trying to find out if the kids made it out. Finally, when they hear their parents' voices, the children emerge from their neighbor's house, trembling and traumatized, clinging to their parents like they never want to let them go.

It's a beautiful reunion, in spite of how terrifying it all was, even as the house continues to burn to the ground. No matter that they're surrounded by ashes. These parents thought they might have lost their kids, and now they are hugging them and crying tears of joy.

Now, imagine a similar scene, but this time the call lets the couple know that their house is on fire. "We think it's only a kitchen fire," the neighbor says, "but the kids are fine. Just get here as fast as you can."

The couple returns home to see that the fire had destroyed the newly remodeled kitchen as well as some important paperwork that was spread out on the table. There's some damage in adjacent rooms, too, and the repairs look extremely costly and long-term. Gazing at the destruction in front of them, the couple feels gutted, thinking, *We've lost almost everything.*

Do you see the difference? There was more damage in the first scenario, but because the parents thought it might have been worse— the loss of their children—they rejoiced to find their kids safe and were relieved that they only lost their home. In the second scenario, the couple was devastated because they were thinking in terms of minimal damage and came home to much worse. Expectations made the difference.

Much of this book so far has dealt with asking the right questions when we go through difficult circumstances. The first is, *Where is my focus?* When you're in the middle of challenging situations—relational, financial, physical, emotional, or anything else—it's easy to turn inward and get discouraged or depressed. To get perspective, you have to ask yourself where your focus is and make sure it's upward and outward.

> Much of this book so far has dealt with asking the right questions when we go through difficult circumstances.

The second question is, *What is my purpose?* Is it just comfort and happiness and making sure everything works out the way you want? Or, is it about how God might leverage your adversity to help people—nonbelievers, believers, and yourself—to know Jesus and grow deeper spiritually? Your sense of purpose will shape how you navigate challenges, and seeing God work out His purposes even in your trials will enable you to rejoice in the midst of them.

The third question is, *Where is my hope?* Is it in a certain job, a marriage or family situation, optimal health, or satisfying experiences in life? Or is it in Jesus and the promise of eternity with Him? When you know you have an unshakable anchor that will not change, shifting circumstances can't steal your joy.

When you ask those big questions, you get perspective. When you realize that God never promised to eliminate your problems or rescue you out of them, but He does promise to help you through them and bring good out of them, then you can live in joy no matter what you go through.

There's one more question we need to ask, and it's the last key to experiencing fullness of joy. It's also one of the most important ones.

GOD'S EXPECTATIONS AND OURS

If you've lived very long at all, you know life is hard. Some people know that better than others. Some have lived through extremely difficult circumstances that have wreaked havoc on relationships, finances, or health. As much as we long for a problem-free existence, we will almost certainly go through difficulties and pain. Challenges are just part of life in a fallen world.

I don't want to give the impression that it's all bad. God gives us seasons—sometimes very long ones—that are filled with wonderful blessings and are fully satisfying. He promises His goodness every day of our lives. When Jesus told His followers that they would have tribulation in this world, He did not mean they would have nothing but tribulation. Not at all. But anyone who thinks we're going to get through life without pain is mistaken.

> Few things undermine our joy more than the false expectation that "life shouldn't be hard"

I also don't want to give the impression that choosing joy is all about willpower—that if we just discipline ourselves to do it, it will happen. That's not how this works. As we have seen, this involves a reorientation of our perspective over time. It doesn't happen overnight, but if we immerse ourselves in truth and choose an eternal perspective, we eventually learn to see life not through a human lens but through a divine lens. We anchor ourselves in eternity and live with the focus, purpose, and hope that brings us joy.

Few things undermine our joy more than the false expectation that "life shouldn't be hard"—that even if we go through difficult times, God will deliver us out of them or bring us through without pain and perseverance. I remember playing golf with a new acquaintance who had been wrestling with these kinds of expectations. He was a nice, successful businessman, and he and his wife had a God-given desire to care for international kids, so they adopted three children from China. It was a very loving thing to do, and they assumed it would bring God's blessing and favor. It did, of course, but blessing and favor didn't look like this couple expected. All of the children had medical and emotional issues and were going through counseling. Two of the children required significant surgeries accompanied by high medical bills. It took everything they had to keep going.

"I didn't know if our marriage was going to make it," he told me. "And I don't know if I would have done what we did if I'd known how hard it was. My expectations were way off, and it took me several years to realize that. The time, money, pain, and emotional energy we put into this have made it really hard."

My heart went out to him. They had been through a lot, and all of it was from good, pure intentions to serve God and love others. Some people go through that experience and become very disillusioned, blaming God or each other. This couple was eventually able to work through it. By the time I talked with him, he could say, "I know it was worth it." And he was able to say it with a smile.

KEY #4: Expectations
QUESTION #4: What are my expectations?

SETTING EXPECTATIONS

The fourth key to choosing joy is expectations, and the fourth question we need to ask is, *What are my expectations?* What do you expect from God? Most of our expectations are usually unconscious—we're hardly aware of them until reality confronts us with contradictions to them—so this isn't an easy question to answer. But you have them. We all do.

Some of the more common ones go something like this: *If you love Jesus, your marriage will be great. If you're single, the right person is going to walk into your life. If you love Jesus and think positive thoughts, everything is going to work out. If you sacrificially support God's work financially, He will always give you more than you think you need. If you parent your children according to biblical values and principles, they will all grow up to be strong believers.* You get the picture.

If you don't have clear, accurate, biblical expectations, you can be living a really blessed life but still be miserable because you unconsciously think it should be a more perfect one. I learned this the hard way during one of the darkest times of marital struggle Theresa and I went through. I'd gone into our marriage with very skewed expectations, and it led to a lot of unrealistic attitudes. We both loved God, were "sold out to Jesus" and committed to full-time ministry. We had kept our relationship sexually pure prior to marriage and rarely had an argument before we got married. I was *expecting* a problem-free, greatly blessed, sexually fulfilling, amazing life. After our first argument, I thought I married the wrong person. Communication challenges, our past baggage, family-of-origin issues, and honest differences in personality made for challenge after challenge that almost destroyed us. During this time, I read a quote by Francis Schaeffer: "We do not need to cast away every human relationship, including the relationship of marriage, or the relationships of Christians inside the church, just because they prove not to be perfect."[5] We are all vulnerable to that dynamic if we aren't clear on what to expect from life.

Don't get me wrong. Expectations in themselves are not bad. Faith is an expectation, and we can't please God without it. But there are realistic expectations and unfounded expectations, and often a fine line between them, and we tend to cross that line easily and unconsciously. God does give us promises regarding marriage, family, children, finances, prayer, health, and much more. We should absolutely believe them. But there's a difference between believing them as God means them and believing them for what we want them to say. And that's where we often trip up.

I think this is why so many Christians are disillusioned. The distance between your expectations and your experience is disappointment. If your expectations are unrealistic or unfounded, the result can be devastating.

The distance between your expectations and your experience is disappointment.

Paul shows us very specifically what we can expect from God—and what He expects of us. Remember, Paul is under house arrest, at least figuratively in chains and sometimes literally chained to praetorian guards, wondering whether he is going to be released or executed. These are not pleasant circumstances, but he has an upward and outward focus, is grounded in his purpose, and has a certain hope rooted in eternity. As much as he longs to be with Jesus face-to-face, he is also deeply concerned for believers like the Philippians, who are experiencing some external opposition and internal disunity. So, in his final thoughts in the first chapter of his letter to this church, Paul wants to set clear expectations: *This is what God expects of you in terms of your behavior, your beliefs, and your boldness. And here is what you should expect from God.*

First, here's what God expects: "Only conduct yourselves in a manner worthy of the gospel of Christ" (Phil. 1:27).

The word for "only" carries the sense of "above all" (NLT) or "whatever happens" (NIV), suggesting that this is a priority. At all costs, believers should live this way. "In a manner worthy" (*axios*) is an interesting word that would resonate with the Philippians based on their experience as a Roman colony. The city had been made a Roman colony after Octavian (later Caesar Augustus) won a major battle there against Julius Caesar's assassins in 42 BC, and with colonization came rights, privileges, and responsibilities of citizenship for many of Philippi's residents. Those rights, privileges, and responsibilities included access to newly constructed roads and aqueducts, as well as conforming to Roman laws and paying Roman taxes. It involved alignment with the Roman way of life.

Not all Christians in Philippi would have been Roman citizens, but all would have understood the implications of citizenship. And by using a word that suggests that kind of civic responsibility, Paul is giving his readers an illustration relevant to their own lives. In the same way Roman citizens conform to Roman culture, citizens of God's kingdom should conform to kingdom culture—at all costs. That means even as they are enduring pressure and opposition, the same conflicts Paul is experiencing (v. 30), they should also embrace the perspectives and values of heaven as he is doing. In other words, they need to be Christians who act like Christians.

That's an extremely relevant message for our times, in case you didn't notice. In fact, it has become a mission statement for our ministry: to challenge and equip Christians to live like Christians.

Research has shown Western churches are in decline—the numbers of Christians who believe the Bible and authentically follow Jesus are much smaller than most surveys suggest—and the solution is genuine, committed discipleship. This is how God changes the world—by transforming people who will truly follow Jesus and teach others to follow Him too.

Paul is essentially telling the Philippians to be careful not to become Christians who don't act like Christians. Not only should their words say they love Jesus; their values, behavior, morality, priorities, and relationships should tell the same story. There should be alignment between what they say and how they live. Christians are to conduct themselves in a manner worthy of the gospel.

So, lest we gloss over the implications of this command for our lives, take a moment to think about who or what you're struggling with right now, and then apply this verse to that situation. This kind of alignment is how God expects you to approach that issue, situation, or person. God wants you to bring gospel values and behaviors into that situation or relationship. When you do, you'll discover an interesting phenomenon. When you obey God, things begin to change. He changes what happens on the inside of you and will provide what you need in that situation or relationship. Again, He doesn't always miraculously deliver you out of a problem, but He does work within it and deliver you through it.

UNDERSTANDING EXPECTATIONS

Paul's statement raises immediate questions. *What does that look like? How can you know if you're consistently living like a kingdom citizen?* After all, he isn't writing to people who have the four gospels and Acts and all of his letters bound in a leather cover with handy verse references for them to look up. They are among the pioneers of the church, and Scripture to them is the Old Testament—which, as gentiles, most of them are still beginning to grasp. So, what does it mean to live in a manner worthy of the gospel?

Paul tells them: "So that whether I come and see you or remain absent, I will hear of you that you are standing firm in one spirit, with one mind striving together for the faith of the gospel; in no way alarmed by your opponents—which is a sign of destruction for them, but of salvation for you, and that too, from God" (Phil. 1:27–28).

In essence, Paul is telling them that whether he lives or dies—he still isn't sure of the outcome, even though he has said he believes he will continue on in the flesh—he will probably still at least hear about them, and he wants to hear three specific things that indicate whether they are living consistently aligned with God's purposes.

Don't Give Up

Whether Paul comes to the Philippians in person or hears about them from afar, he wants to know that they are "standing firm in one spirit." In other words, he is telling them not to give up.

Have you ever felt like giving up? It's easy to feel that way—and in many situations:

- You've tried making a stand on an important issue, but you keep running into a wall of opposition.
- You've tried to stick it out at your job or in your marriage, but you've lost hope that anything is ever going to change.
- You've tried maintaining a strong Christian witness in a culture that increasingly looks down on Christians, and you wonder if you're having any impact at all.
- You know what the Bible says about sexual purity, but today's media, psychological interpretations of sexuality,

and your own physiology rage against the restraints of biblical teaching.

- You've consistently tithed and tried to steward your finances well, but it's getting harder and harder to pay the bills, and you don't know how to get by without cutting corners and compromising commitments.

Sometimes the forces against you seem to be stronger than the faith inside you, and you just want to give up.

Paul says, "Don't." Yes, it's difficult to be a Christian and live out biblical values in today's world, but it was just as difficult for the Philippian believers as a small religious minority in an idol-worshiping, sex-saturated, politically pragmatic culture. It has never been easy in any era. The answer is not to give up; it's to keep drawing closer to God and tap into the power He puts within you. Difficulties and pain cause some people to leave the faith and others to lean in to it even further. That's Paul's instruction here. Lean in, even when it's hard.

The core issue here is not simply perseverance. It's whether we really believe and trust God. When you take a stand, feel stuck, lose a job, and take hits to your reputation for your faith, do you believe and trust Him to take care of you and orchestrate your circumstances? When an employer demands hours that don't allow you to be who you need to be for your family, do you trust God enough to set some boundaries or go somewhere else? When you find yourself in situations that demand compromise, are you willing to live like a believer by God's grace and power without caving in? Those are trust issues.

When you trust Him like that, you become a light in this world and the salt of the earth (Matt. 5:13–16). That's the kind of lifestyle that makes a difference, even when you don't see the difference it is making. At some point, someone will. God will honor your faithfulness. But you have to stand firm and not give up in order to have the impact He wants you to have.

A lot of Christians have forgotten that. Most people in our society today see very few differences between the average Christian and the average non-Christian. They see our priorities, our behavior, our morality and ethics, and many of them are thinking, *If it's not any different, why should I follow Jesus?* God is doing some amazing things through believers and churches that remain faithful—that follow Paul's instructions to live in a manner worthy of the gospel and not give up. My prayer for me and for you is that we will be faithful as well, regardless of the cost.

Don't Give In

In addition to standing firm in one spirit, the Philippians are to strive together with one mind. Those two instructions might sound very similar, even redundant, but there's a subtle difference between them. One is about maintaining their position without giving up. The other is about advancing, contending for the faith without giving in. Various translations phrase this differently: "striving side by side" (Phil. 1:27 ESV), "striving together as one" (NIV), "fighting together" (NLT), but they are all about laboring together, struggling together, advancing together in one mind—literally, as "one soul." They are to function as one organism, one life, one body with many parts.

This is not about private faith. In individualistic cultures, we make faith a personal issue—"to each his own"—that we live out separately even if we meet together once or twice a week. The image Paul presents here is of gladiators going out arm-in-arm to fight against the opposition—in this case, a battle for the truth that Jesus is God, the second person of the Trinity, who became a man, died, and rose from the dead to give us new life. In places like Philippi, Judaism and Christianity were seen as strange Eastern religions. The idea that there is one God revealed through one people in a historical narrative that spans centuries and culminates in a sacrificial death and resurrection seemed very foreign and even crazy to Romans and Greeks. Paul was telling the believers in this city, "I want you to contend for this faith."

Don't misunderstand. He is not telling them to go out and fight nonbelievers physically or even figuratively. Some Christians then and now misunderstand the mission. They bring heat, not light. Paul wants these Philippians to win this battle "in a manner worthy of the gospel"—lovingly, winsomely, and with rock-solid conviction of the truth. That pairing—truth and love—combines acts and words of compassion and kindness with uncompromising faith in the gospel and God's presence and power in believers' lives.

Our polarized society gives us numerous opportunities to do that today. Public discourse is filled with so many hot-button issues and aggressive opinions that anyone who addresses those issues reasonably, compassionately, understandingly, and sensitively will almost certainly stand out. Many people address issues like abortion, gender, and social justice with an attitude of righteous anger. What if we discuss them while expressing God's heart—that He has given us biblical truth to heal us, redeem and restore us, and give us rich and satisfying lives? God has compassion for everyone who has distorted perspectives on important issues like these. In most cases, what they really want is acceptance, kindness, fairness, equality, and fulfillment. Their answers just aren't going to accomplish that. God's truth will. If it is shared with a loving heart without compromising what the Scripture says, some people might actually see Him for who He is and receive the truth He has given us.

I recently saw a man waiting around at the end of one of our services like he wasn't sure about being there. Finally, he asked, "Am I welcome here?"

"What do you mean?" I asked. "Of course you're welcome here."

"Well, I'm gay," he told me.

"Okay. Is that a behavior or an identity? We have people here who struggle with all kinds of temptations—pornography, lying, stealing, extramarital affairs, greed. People with all kinds of issues are welcome here. We have people in our church that are highly attracted to the opposite sex, but that's a temptation, not an identity. So, you are as welcome here as those who come with other struggles like lying, cheating, sexual addictions, affairs, pornography, and unresolved anger. We come to a God who meets us where we are and has rescued and is rescuing us from those things; but we all come in with something."

> Jesus welcomes all of us to come to Him as we are. He meets us where we are but refuses to leave us stuck in our issues.

Jesus welcomes all of us to come to Him as we are. He meets us where we are but refuses to leave us stuck in our issues. The new life He offers begins a lifelong journey to transform us into His likeness. We trust that God will speak to people and change their thinking and their lives from the inside out.

We have a number of followers in our church who have struggled with same-sex attraction and have experienced forgiveness and freedom from their homosexual lifestyle. We would love to have anyone come and explore God's love and plan for their lives. Some people aren't comfortable with the idea that they need any kind of change at all. In fact, talking about identity issues the way we do can get you fired or canceled in some places. But deep down, most people know they need change, and Christians who invitingly, lovingly approach life as a transformative, disciple-making process have an impact on their culture. They may take a lot of hits from the opposition, but they also open some hearts to the truth.

Churches and denominations across our country are giving in by changing their doctrine because it has become increasingly unpopular to believe what Jesus actually said. Through his instructions to the Philippians, Paul urges us not to give in—to know the truth and stake our lives on it. God is calling us to do the same; to not give in, to stick together, single-mindedly—as one.

Don't Shrink Back

Paul is aware that the Philippian believers have "enemies"—they live in a culture that is hostile to the gospel—so he tells them not to be intimidated or alarmed. The word here is sometimes used for a sudden sight or sound that might spook horses and provoke a stampede. He doesn't want the Philippians to be spooked like that. In the face of opposition, they need to know who they are as citizens of God's kingdom—a much higher culture than the one that opposes them—and not shrink back.

Some Christians love a good culture war; most prefer not to make waves. But there's a lot of room to have positive influence between those two reactions, not simply for the sake of the culture, but for the sake of the kingdom. Vast numbers of believers today disagree with vocal minorities who are shaping our culture, but don't speak up because they don't want to deal with the consequences. We need to remember that beyond politics and culture wars, we're called to advance the gospel—to proclaim the gift of salvation and the life-transforming power of Jesus. That's what's at stake.

That was Paul's focus. A few years before he wrote to the Philippians, Paul wrote to the Romans that he was "not ashamed of the gospel, for it is the power of God for salvation to everyone who believes" (Rom. 1:16). In other words, "I'm not going to shrink back." That's exactly the attitude he wants the Philippians to have. He doesn't want them to bow down to whatever is politically correct, compromise their beliefs to appease their bosses or customers, or go silent when their city tells them to be quiet. Those are hard words in a society where their livelihood might be affected by the biases against them, but again, this is a matter of trust. Can God take care of someone who stands up for truth and refuses to shrink back? Scripture and experience show that He can. Paul wants the Philippians to bank on that trust.

I've lived for more than twenty-five years in the most progressive and pro-LGBTQ+ regions of America, and I can tell you story after story of fellow believers (workers and executives) at Google, Facebook, VMware, Intel, and Apple who have maintained their testimony, been openly Christian, and made a huge difference in their companies. They have refused to "shrink back" and at the same time treated those who oppose them with dignity and kindness, and worked with such integrity and excellence, that they've earned the respect of those in the LGBTQ+ community. It takes courage to stand up for what one believes, and it takes humility to genuinely listen to where others are coming from and treat them as fellow human beings whose perspective and values may be far different than yours, but who are made in the image of God and demand your utmost respect. One does not have to compromise one's faith or convictions to treat people the way the apostle Paul commands us (2 Tim. 2:24–25).

These instructions are for us too. Eternity is on the line. Souls are at stake. The consequences of people turning away from God are devastating. People need to hear the clarion call of truth expressed in love and see both truth and love in the lives of those who follow Jesus. It's a high calling and a hard one, but it's vital. Don't shrink back.

Those are the three specific ways you can live in a manner worthy of the gospel. Don't give up, don't give in, and don't shrink back. Base those postures on the truth, of course—there are a lot of believers out there who don't give up, give in, or shrink back in attitudes and behaviors that don't express the nature of Christ and the heart of God. "The Lord's bond-servant must not be quarrelsome, but be kind to all, able to teach, patient when wronged, with gentleness correcting those who are in opposition, if perhaps God may grant them repentance leading to the knowledge of the truth" (2 Tim. 2:24–25).

As citizens of the kingdom of God, we demonstrate the character and nature of the King. That's our calling. It's not exceptional; it's normal Christianity, and we are to stand firm, press forward, and live it out with commitment and boldness.

When we do that, Paul says, it becomes a "sign," a token, proof that demonstrates our future and the future of those who oppose us (Phil. 1:28). When we as believers live in contrast to our culture, our different lifestyle becomes a demonstration of a different future—that when God separates the saved from the unsaved, the distinctions will make sense because they weren't hard to see. False worldviews, teachings, and values will ultimately be destroyed, and truth will ultimately be vindicated.

ARE YOU STANDING FIRM TOGETHER?

How are you doing in standing firm and striving together without fear? How do you feel about the church as a whole on these points?

I think most Christians would agree with Paul's instructions, but when pressed, would admit that they aren't living them out very well. Some are more worried about being a citizen of their country than about being a citizen of God's kingdom, even when they know kingdom citizenship should be their priority. It's human nature to want to be comfortable and content, and living a normal Christian life as Paul presents it (as opposed to a "normal" Christian life as our culture presents it) is rarely comfortable or easy. But we were made for eternity, and our time is running out. It's time for us, every follower of Jesus, to not *give up,* not *give in,* and not *shrink back.*

I think God is calling us to a new level of boldness. I believe He wants to reawaken His church and move powerfully through His people around the world. It isn't enough for people just to know we're Christians. He wants us to live like Christians boldly—not irritatingly or obnoxiously, but with conviction and confidence. He wants us to be filled with joy and for our joy to be a testimony to those around us.

God is calling us to enter the most unwelcoming, un-Christian environments and share the love of Jesus without fear and without compromise.

> Ask God to speak to you about whether your beliefs and your behavior are telling the same story

Christians who aren't afraid to say "Jesus" out loud. Christians who will approach people who are hostile to the gospel, look them in the eyes, listen to their stories, and talk about how God sees today's issues without preaching or condemning. Believers who are willing to say, "Yes, we're followers of Christ. We love people. It's true, we believe certain things that are unpopular today, and here's why . . ." Christians who know that there's power in the name of Jesus and beauty in His character, and that people are drawn to Him through their ministry. That's what it looks like in our day to live in a manner worthy of the gospel.

When you live that kind of life, you'll probably face some more pressure and experience a bit more pain. But you'll also have a much greater impact. God will use you as a catalyst to transform your family, your neighborhood, your workplace, your church, and wherever else you have influence.

Ask God to speak to you about whether your beliefs and your behavior are telling the same story—whether or not you're living in a manner worthy of the gospel without compromise or fear. Pray that He would increase your boldness and your sensitivity to speak the truth in love to those around you. Ask Him to make you an agent of the kingdom, a catalyst for transformation, as He works in people's lives. And trust that as you offer Him what He expects of you, He will work powerfully in you and through you. He will give you plenty of reasons to choose joy.

DISCUSSION/APPLICATION QUESTIONS

1. The first two stories in this chapter are all about expectations and how we respond, depending on what our expectations are. What personal example could you add to those stories?

2. What does the apostle Paul teach in Philippians 1:27–28 that God expects of us as faithful believers in a hostile world?

3. In what ways are you currently tempted to "give up," "give in," or "shrink back" because of challenging circumstances or cultural pressures in your life?

4. In what one specific relationship could you bring God's truth and love with light and not heat to someone far from God?

Assignment: Sometimes the most challenging calling from God in difficult situations with difficult people is simply to persevere. Jot the promise below in the box and make it your screensaver on your phone or computer all this week.

> After you have suffered for a little while, the God of all grace, who called you to His eternal glory in Christ, will Himself perfect, confirm, strengthen and establish you.
>
> (1 Peter 5:10)

CHAPTER 8:

How to Realign Your Expectations

Two words rarely appear in the same sentence: *joy* and *suffering*. There's likely a number of reasons, but for most of us, joy is so strongly associated with what makes us feel happy, and what is associated with positive circumstances, that the thought of joy in suffering is a foreign concept.

In addition, the proliferation of the prosperity gospel in recent decades has created a sharp divide between being in God's will and suffering. Although Jesus promised that we would suffer and that tribulation would be a normal part of our faith journey (John 16:33), the popular ideas that "right living and lots of faith" will produce a stress-free, worry-free, financially prosperous life has sunk its roots deeply into the global evangelical mindset.

Be forewarned that this final chapter talks about some "graduate-level joy." Together we're going to learn that we can experience joy in the midst of even life's most challenging and difficult times.

I confess, this is not something I learned early in my walk with

God. In fact, I remember my first real experience of meeting someone who experienced overwhelming joy in the midst of severe suffering. It was in Hong Kong more than thirty years ago. I was teaching a pastors' conference and had the opportunity to eat dinner with a pastor who had traveled from China. As the night unfolded, he shared how he and his wife were leading a house church, and while he was away traveling, the police raided the church and took his wife into custody. She convinced them that she was the pastor, and for three days she was held in jail and beaten several times. As he told the story, my blood began to boil as I thought of my response to a similar situation if that was my wife, Theresa.

> Until that point in my life, I'd never heard someone describe the incredible joy of any experience associated with suffering.

Just about the time my righteous anger was ready to boil over, a smile lit up across his face and tears began to well up in his eyes as he said, "Can you imagine the joy and privilege it was for her to get to suffer for Jesus?" My jaw dropped as his words began to sink into my mind. Until that point in my life, I'd never heard someone describe the incredible joy of any experience associated with suffering.

Fast-forward many years later, God launched the Living on the Edge radio broadcast. It began in the San Francisco Bay Area and then spread across the country with God opening doors in stations and cities all across America. A devout nun with a deep love for Jesus found our broadcast and recorded it on a cassette player every morning at 5 a.m. She would then pass on the cassette to her Mother Superior and all the nuns would listen to the message.

Over time, I learned that her name was Sister Mary of the Holy Spirit, and she began to write me regularly and share poems that the Lord gave her to share with others. Her calling was in a cloistered convent that she entered at age nineteen and was only permitted to leave one day a year. I met her when she was in her late eighties and suffering from very severe physical challenges.

I'll never forget the day that Theresa and I decided to go visit Sister Mary. We went to the convent, and there was a special window with some bars where she could sit on one side and we could sit on the other as we made conversation and shared life with one another. Of course, we had our differences, and she occasionally would write me letters about some of my messages that weren't quite right in her eyes as I talked about Jesus' mother. However, our common love for Jesus built a bond over the years that was very precious.

As we were talking, I noticed a very large lump on the back of her neck and at the base of her skull. I asked her about it and learned that it was something she's lived with for many years and with much pain. When I inquired about how I might be of help to get it "fixed," she let me know that there was no medical solution, but that this condition had been a very special joy for her to suffer for Jesus and with Him. She began to tear up and talk about the intimacy that she has experienced because of the pain, which allowed her to participate in some small way with identifying with the pain of Jesus on our behalf. Sister Mary of the Holy Spirit was one of the most joyful people I had ever met, and she radiated the love of Christ in her smile, her countenance, and her great devotion in serving others.

Please don't get lost in the details of this story or go down a theological cul-de-sac right now and miss the real point of this story. Despite the official position of the Roman Catholic Church, it was obvious from my multiple years of interaction with Sister Mary of the Holy Spirit that she had a very deep and personal relationship with Jesus by faith in His grace. What I want you to appreciate is that the Bible is very clear that joy and suffering are not incompatible. In fact, the writer of Hebrews reminds us of Jesus' perspective: "Who, for the joy set before him, endured the cross, despising the shame, and sat down at the right hand of the throne of God" (Heb. 12:2).

> **What I want you to appreciate is that the Bible is very clear that joy and suffering are not incompatible.**

And now lest we get stuck in the weeds of the other extreme, as though the deeper spiritual life is about hurt, pain, and suffering, and the only way to experience the joy of the Lord is through some willful and distorted desire to suffer, let's look at a number of great promises that God has for all of us.

THE GIFT OF SUFFERING

God has filled His Word with numerous promises and assurances, and as His children and co-heirs of His kingdom, we have every reason to believe them all. He is presented throughout Scripture as the Giver of good gifts—our Savior, Healer, Deliverer, Comforter, Provider, and more. Jesus told us that He came for us to have life "abundantly" (John 10:10). These are the expectations God's own Word creates for us, and there's nothing wrong with embracing them fully.

But Scripture also sets us up for some other expectations that surprise many people. After telling the Philippians what God expects of them, He tells them what they can expect from God: "For to you it has been granted for Christ's sake, not only to believe in Him, but also to suffer for His sake, experiencing the same conflict which you saw in me, and now hear to be in me" (Phil. 1:29–30).

The word *granted* (*charizomai*) comes from a familiar word for "grace" (*charis*). It literally means that God has given us a privilege. He has favored us with this gift not only of believing in Jesus, but also of suffering for His sake. According to Paul, that's what the Philippians can expect from God. He isn't saying this is *all* they can expect from God—again, remember all of God's promises and assurances given to His children—but in the context of their increasing boldness, as they refuse to give up, give in, and shrink back, this is an outcome that should not surprise them. They will have to endure some pushback, and it won't be comfortable or easy.

We might not think of suffering as a gift, and the Philippians probably didn't either. But in keeping with the theme of citizenship, which many of Philippi's residents enjoyed by virtue of the city's status as a Roman colony, citizens of God's kingdom have certain privileges and responsibilities. And believing in Jesus and suffering for the sake of Jesus are two of them. They are both privileges and responsibilities.

In pointing out these two gifts of grace, Paul is essentially telling the believers in this church, "Remember your citizenship in God's kingdom? Here's what it means. You've been given the priceless privilege of believing in Jesus and receiving eternal life. He has loved you, chosen you, changed you, transferred you from the kingdom of darkness into the kingdom of light, placed you in His own family, sealed you with His Spirit, given you a purpose, and promised you an eternity with Him in heaven." Not all of those concepts are in this passage, but they are all in Paul's letters. This is how he describes the privilege of believing in Jesus.

Paul is also telling them, "Now God is going to transform your life to make you more and more like Jesus, and since Jesus suffered for boldly speaking the truth in love in order to save a dying world, you're also going to suffer as you boldly speak the truth in love." That's the second gift. You get to suffer.

REJOICING IN SUFFERING

Acts 5 tells the story of how Jewish authorities in Jerusalem arrested some of the apostles for teaching in the name of Jesus—they especially didn't like the part about how these leaders had unjustly called for His crucifixion—and eventually flogged them and sent them away with another warning not to preach in Jesus' name. What was the apostles' response? "They went on their way from the presence of the Council, rejoicing that they had been considered worthy to suffer shame for His name" (Acts 5:41).

Rejoicing in suffering? That seems like a foreign concept for most Western Christians today. In some parts of the world, believers understand this concept very well. But most of us who have lived in relatively free societies have never learned to see persecution as a privilege. We miss the ways it connects us with Jesus and demonstrates His life within us.

The night before Jesus' crucifixion, He told His disciples that they could find peace in Him. They would need it. Why? Because "in the world you have tribulation," He said. "But take courage; I have overcome the world" (John 16:33).

When Paul wrote to encourage Timothy in his role as pastor in Ephesus, he reminded him of the truth that "all who desire to live godly in Christ Jesus will be persecuted" (2 Tim. 3:12). What would you think if your mentor or supervisor said, "I've got a job for you. It's in a really crazy city, but I think you can reach a lot of people there. But I want you to know that if you do your job well and with integrity, you'll be persecuted." That's basically what Paul told Timothy. It wasn't speculation. It was reality.

These are promises. They are just as real as God's promises for answered prayer and an eternity with Him in heaven. Paul understood that, and he wanted to help set his readers' expectations.

If we keep reading into the second chapter of Philippians, we find that Paul presents Jesus as the perfect example of the attitude these believers should have. Just as Jesus left heaven, emptied Himself of the privileges of deity, took on the form of a servant even to the point of death, and then was exalted and honored by God (Phil. 2:6–11), we should have the same humility. We often think of this passage as a separate section in the letter, but remember that the original had no chapters, verses, or, in many cases, even any paragraph breaks. This ultimate example flows out of Paul's instructions in chapter 1 and the first few verses of chapter 2. If the Philippians wanted to know what it looked like to suffer for boldly speaking and living out the truth in love, they needed to look no further than Jesus.

In the days before Jesus told the disciples they would have tribulation in this world, He delivered an unpopular sermon to hypocritical religious leaders about them being like snakes and whitewashed tombs; He promised judgment on Jerusalem; and He talked about tumultuous times when there would be false prophets, wars and rumors of war, and famines and earthquakes. He assured His followers that some of them would be arrested, persecuted, and killed, and through it all, they should never be ashamed of Him (Luke 9:26). Believers should persevere in their faith and not be afraid.

Some of the original disciples had already experienced that, and because Jesus had warned them, they even leaned into the suffering. Paul warned the Philippians that opposition was coming because he didn't want them to be surprised when they suffered too. He had essentially told them in the previous verses to be politically incorrect as needed in order to present the truth of the gospel. But he knew the repercussions. Jesus was the most politically incorrect teacher we can imagine, and look what happened to Him. To one degree or another, this is how life works for followers of Jesus.

The early church understood this. According to tradition, Peter was crucified upside down because he didn't think he was worthy to be crucified in the same manner as Jesus. Some of the greatest periods of growth in the first three hundred years of the church were when pandemics ravaged entire populations and Christians demonstrated love for the sick, even at the risk of their own lives. By the time the emperor Constantine legalized Christianity in AD 313, Christians had grown from a small group of disciples to about 10 percent of the population (about 6 million), not because they were such persuasive speakers and evangelists, but because they lived a radical lifestyle, even when they suffered for it. Many people were so moved by their commitment and perseverance that they began to ask what their faith was all about. Suffering played a key role in the growth of the church and by AD 350 it is estimated that more than 50 percent (33 million) of the Roman Empire were Christians.[6]

> **According to tradition, Peter was crucified upside down because he didn't think he was worthy to be crucified in the same manner as Jesus.**

Some of the "birth pangs" Jesus talked about (Matt. 24:8) are evident in our times. They have been evident in many other periods of history, too, so I'm not making any predictions about when the end will come. But the dynamics of the kingdom are always true, and believers are always subject to opposition while we live out eternal truth in this temporal world. The warnings in Scripture are for every generation. They tell us to live with awareness and urgency; to live out the gospel boldly; not to fear for our jobs, reputations, or lives; and to persevere even in the face of a culture that thinks we're crazy and wants to punish us for the way we think. From what we know of history, that kind of testimony can change the culture.

When Paul was writing to the Philippians from Rome, Christians in Rome were likely not being severely persecuted. Many Jewish Christians had been expelled in AD 49—not because they were Christians but because they were Jews—and had come back a few years later after Claudius died. Now that Nero was emperor, Christians were simply looked down upon, like they were in many places. That would change a couple years later. When Rome burned, Nero scapegoated Christians and demonstrated his contempt for this sect by burning Christians as torches and sending them to the lions in arenas.

This outbreak of persecution may have been when Peter wrote his first letter to churches across the empire. His message is similar to Paul's and even more direct:

> What credit is there if, when you sin and are harshly treated, you endure it with patience? But if when you do what is right and suffer for it you patiently endure it, this finds favor with God. For you have been called for this purpose, since Christ also suffered for you, leaving you an example for you to follow in His steps. (1 Peter 2:20–21)

From the perspective of Peter and Paul, suffering doesn't just happen occasionally. It's part of the package. It may not be part of the package for every person in all seasons, but it is everyone's experience at some point. And we need to live with that expectation, knowing that some of the earliest followers of Jesus considered it a privilege.

What's the bottom line? There's a visible world and an invisible world, and the invisible world is eternal. Our life on earth is a dot on that endless string we talked about earlier, and we need to live for the entire line, not just the dot. We can't do that unless we understand that suffering in this world is very temporary—Paul called it "momentary" and "light" (2 Cor. 4:17)—and we will live in glory, free from suffering, with Jesus forever.

> **If we try to avoid suffering all the time, we never become the men and women God designed us to be.**

If we try to avoid suffering all the time, we never become the men and women God designed us to be. We never grow fully into the image of Jesus or have the impact we were created and called to have. We miss an important part of our calling.

Are you willing to take that stand? Can you really say, as Paul does (Rom. 1:16), that you are not ashamed of the gospel? Can you live with a testimony of joy even when you get backlash—or any other time that life hurts?

WHY WE SUFFER

I don't want to give the impression that God causes suffering. That doesn't reflect His goodness. Suffering will happen anyway. We live in a fallen world that has rebelled against God's purposes and tried to formulate its own truth. Anyone living on this side of heaven is going to experience the pain and imperfection of this fallen world, and anyone living in the power of the Spirit and advancing God's kingdom is going to experience the hostility of God's enemy. God doesn't cause that.

But He does use it. Suffering is part of this world, and we find at least six specific reasons in Scripture why we experience it. Many have cried out, "Lord, why?! What did I do? Why am I going through this?" The answer is usually one of these reasons:

My Own Sin

When we get angry, lash out, say things we shouldn't . . . when we lie, cheat, or steal . . . when we behave immorally, contrary to God's design . . . when we fill our minds with greed, covetousness, or other selfish desires . . . we shouldn't be surprised to experience unpleasant, painful outcomes. Sin has consequences.

Paul put it this way: "Do not be deceived, God is not mocked; for whatever a man sows, this he will also reap" (Gal. 6:7). If we do dumb things, we experience the results of our stupidity. If we do evil things, we get evil consequences. We often suffer by doing things that result in suffering.

God offers forgiveness for our sins. When we confess and repent for what we've done, when we place our faith in Jesus and His sacrifice for our sins, everything we have done wrong, are doing wrong, and will do wrong, is forgiven. Our slate is wiped clean. But are there still consequences? Of course. Forgiveness puts us in right standing with God, and He does provide healing and restoration as we return to Him, but He doesn't take all the consequences of our actions away. Those consequences can be painful.

I should point out that the law of sowing and reaping is not only a warning; it's an opportunity. If you want to reap a good harvest, sow good seed. That doesn't make you immune from hardship, but God does honor our faithfulness today with fruitfulness tomorrow. We also need to remember how God overcame this principle to save us. We sowed sin and death, but by faith, we reap what Jesus sowed: eternal life. He overcame the law of sowing and reaping in our lives with regard to salvation because we had sown our own destruction and had no way to undo it. Now we get to reap what He has sown. But in the nuts and bolts of everyday life, sowing and reaping is often how things work, and we may suffer when we've sown the seeds of suffering.

Others' Sin

Others' sin affects us all the time, right? It's why we have a world full of lawsuits and wounded or bitter people. Innocent people are killed by drunk drivers and in senseless drive-by shootings. Children are traumatized by physical and sexual abuse that scar them for the rest of their lives. Savings accounts are wiped out by scammers. Accidents happen not out of anyone's intentional evil, but by simple, careless neglect. And every one of us passes on whatever dysfunction we have to the next generation, whether we mean to or not.

David wrote about a familiar friend and companion who betrayed him: "He has put forth his hands against those who were at peace with him; he has violated his covenant. His speech was smoother than butter, but his heart was war; his words were softer than oil, yet they were drawn swords" (Ps. 55:20–21). The whole psalm is about the suffering David experienced from someone who had done him wrong.

The good news is that God redeems our painful circumstances, restores us with His blessings, and even works out our worst situations for our good (Rom. 8:28). In that same psalm that laments a friend's betrayal, David wrote, "Cast your burden upon the LORD and He will sustain you; He will never allow the righteous to be shaken" (Ps. 55:22). Joseph told the brothers who had sold him into slavery, "You meant evil against me, but God meant it for good in order to bring about this present result, to preserve many people alive" (Gen. 50:20). God even took history's most heinous act—the crucifixion of the perfect Son of God—to accomplish salvation for a rebellious world. He is a master restorer. But that doesn't mean we don't suffer in the process.

Spiritual Attack

When you regularly get into God's Word, decide you're going to apply it to your life, submit yourself to the transformation God wants to work within you, commit yourself to the cause of Christ and the advancement of the gospel, and seek His kingdom above all else, things will start happening. Be ready for that. Don't be afraid; the power at work within you is infinitely greater than anything the enemy can do to you (1 John 4:4), and Jesus promised His followers authority over the power of the enemy and protection from what might ultimately harm them (Luke 10:19). But just know that when you advance God's kingdom in this world, you are taking territory the enemy thinks is his, and there will be opposition.

Paul wrote about this spiritual battle in Ephesians 6. There he describes spiritual attacks and how to defend yourself against them by putting on the armor of God (Eph. 6:10–20). Again, this is not something any believer needs to be afraid of. In the passage we've been going through, Paul has just told the Philippians to stand firm, fight, and don't shrink back. He would never advocate fear of enemy attacks or magnifying the enemy's power as some ominous, dreadful force, as some Christians do. But we do need to be aware of the invisible war and be strong in the strength of the Lord. And we need to expect some opposition so we won't be surprised and fall victim to it. Many believers have taken some hits and experienced painful backlash. Frequently, I meet Christians who are convinced they must be out of God's will because the good they are doing seems to be accompanied by unusual difficulty, unseen challenges, and setbacks. In reality, their suffering is a kind of "left-handed compliment." The enemy sees such impact from their lives and ministry that he seeks to discourage, divide, and destroy them. Far from being out of God's will, suffering is often the evidence that we're making a difference.

This Fallen World

Some people once asked Jesus about the Galileans who had been killed, and His answer leveled the playing field for everyone: "Do you suppose that these Galileans were greater sinners than all other Galileans because they suffered this fate? . . . Or do you suppose that those eighteen on whom the tower in Siloam fell and killed them were worse culprits than all the men who live in Jerusalem?" (Luke 13:2, 4). What was He saying? Concrete cracks, wood rots, and buildings fall.

Experiencing tragedy doesn't mean you are more or less righteous than anyone else. In this fallen world, pain and suffering aren't based on merit. If you live in a world where bad things happen, bad things can happen to you.

Does God offer any protection? Of course He does. Psalm 91 is all about how He guards and delivers His people from dangers.

We are not subject to random forces. But we also aren't immune from tragedies. Believers die in earthquakes, hurricanes, fires, and other disasters. We also get sick sometimes. How to balance those two truths—God's protection, which He has often clearly demonstrated, and the dangers that befall everyone—is something of a mystery. All I know is that we're called to trust God, pray for protection and healing, but also understand that we live in a world full of problems and pain. In our fallen world, wood rots, steel rusts, and "accidents" happen that aren't necessarily anyone's fault. That's why our hope and joy must ultimately be placed in the very hope Jesus gave His disciples that last night He was with them. "I go and prepare a place for you . . . that where I am, there you may be also" (John 14:3). Heaven and a perfect world one day is a source of great joy.

> In our fallen world, wood rots, steel rusts, and "accidents" happen that aren't necessarily anyone's fault.

Spiritual Discipline

The writer of Hebrews, quoting Job and Proverbs, reminds us that God, like a good father, disciplines those He loves (Heb. 12:5–11). Again, it's important not to make God the active agent of suffering here. But He does allow adversity because sometimes that is the very thing that will accomplish His purposes.

For example, as Paul has already shown us, God didn't have Paul arrested in Jerusalem and sent to Rome for trial. Those were enemies of the gospel. But Paul is still confident that God is using his imprisonment to advance the gospel, in spite of those who opposed him. God knows how to get our attention through circumstances that evil enemies, unwitting humans, or the dangers of a fallen world have inflicted on us.

> God speaks to us more clearly through the megaphone of our pain than through the whispers of our pleasure.

I had a number of major sports-related injuries and untimely illnesses at the peak of my college sports career. The frequency and timing eventually got my attention. I was proud, arrogant, and basketball had become an idol. Like a good father, God allowed these setbacks to get my attention, refine my character, grow my faith, and prepare me for future service. I hated it, I struggled, and I was angry. Eventually, I looked in the mirror and reevaluated my life and priorities. Today, I reflect with overwhelming gratitude at how kind my heavenly Father was to not allow me to keep worshiping that which could never fulfill or satisfy. Ironically, once that issue was resolved and I put God first, He allowed me to take my love for the sport and play basketball all around the world, sharing the hope and new life possible in our Lord Jesus Christ.

Sometimes when we're pleading with God to take us out of our circumstances, He's patiently speaking another message: "I'm trying to get your attention because I love you. I want you to look upward so we can address this issue." That issue may be pride, greed, lust, ignoring Him, taking Him for granted, choosing to be blind to our own dysfunction, or any number of other problems we might face. We all have something, don't we? And we all have a Father who wants to help us. Sometimes, as C. S. Lewis put it in *The Problem of Pain*, God speaks to us more clearly through the megaphone of our pain than through the whispers of our pleasure.[7]

Spiritual Development

Paul had experienced extraordinary revelation and encounters with God, but apparently his spiritual depth put him at risk of becoming proud. So, he was given "a thorn in the flesh" to keep him humble (2 Cor. 12:7). As we noted earlier, this may have been a physical ailment or human adversaries—scholars debate the possibilities because the term he used can have different meanings—but in either case, he was suffering. This was not a pleasant thorn. In fact, Paul calls it "a messenger of Satan to torment [him]." But it reminded Paul of how dependent on God he was, and it also revealed a truth that he would not have learned otherwise: God's power is made manifest in the weaknesses of those who depend on Him. So instead of persisting in prayer for relief—something he had likely done with success many times before—Paul learned to be content.

Suffering is God's gift to accomplish His ultimate good in a fallen world. Seems crazy, right? Hardly anyone would consider it a privilege to suffer for the name of Jesus, but those who understand what that name represents learn to do so. When we suffer, we look up, develop compassion for others, quit being so judgmental, learn that life is not "all about me," and follow in the footsteps of Jesus—enduring the discomfort and hostility of this world in order to bring the message of salvation to it.

> Suffering is God's gift to accomplish His ultimate good in a fallen world.

One of my heroines whom I told you about earlier, Joni Eareckson Tada, expressed this truth in a powerful way: "God permits what he hates to achieve what he loves."[8] That's an amazing statement, especially coming from someone who has endured as much pain as she has. Learn from her example. Suffering is the ultimate test case. If you can have joy in pain and adversity, you can have joy in anything.

I don't want to end a book on a downer, but if you think about it, this is Paul's point. He has demonstrated it again and again throughout the first chapter of this letter to the Philippians. The entire letter is infused with joy, and Paul demonstrates the dynamics of rejoicing right from the start. Even in difficult circumstances, even as his ministry seems to be at a standstill (it wasn't—the letters written during this time will change the world), even as he is surrounded by pagan authorities and Christian critics, and even as he warns the Philippians that they will suffer for standing firm, fighting together, and refusing to be intimidated, joy permeates his words.

Choosing joy is a mindset and a lifestyle. It isn't just a matter of willpower and perseverance; it's a new way of thinking and seeing. But if you're in a difficult situation right now and want to begin making that choice in the midst of it, I'd encourage you to pray something like this:

Lord, You know my pain. You also know how You want to work in it and through me to accomplish Your purposes. I pray that my faithfulness would become a powerful testimony to the people around me—that I would stand firm, contend for truth, express it in love, and not shrink back. Help me see Jesus as the hope of glory and live for eternity. Help me see myself the way You do. Help me grasp how much You love me. And as I learn to live with focus, purpose, hope, and true expectations, I pray that You would fill me with joy. That is my choice today and every day. Amen.

DISCUSSION/APPLICATION QUESTIONS

1. What is your emotional reaction to Paul's words in Philippians 1:29—that it is not only a gift to believe in Christ, but also to suffer for His sake?

2. Who do you know that has modeled a genuine joy in their life, despite going through significant trials or suffering? How has their life impacted you?

3. Not all suffering has the same cause. How does understanding the five reasons for suffering help you discern what God may be doing/allowing in your life? Which of the following may be at work in your life right now and why?

- your own sin?
- others' sin?
- spiritual attack?
- this fallen world?
- spiritual development?

4. One source of Paul's joy in his imprisonment and suffering was the prayers of the Philippian church and the presence of Timothy and Epaphroditus. Who could you call today and share what's really going on in your heart?

Assignment: We all tend to repress, hide, or deny the pain and challenges that we are facing. We were never designed to carry these alone, and God's power and presence comes from His Word, His Spirit, and His people.

> • Write a short prayer to God expressing how you really feel, what is bothering you the most, and what you're asking Him to do.

> • Sit quietly and ask the Holy Spirit to give you clear direction on how to respond to your current difficult circumstance or relationship. He promises that if we are willing to do whatever He says, He will make clear what the next step should be (James 1:5–7).

> • Make a call or text today to someone you trust who is spiritually mature and ask if they will get coffee with you this week. Share with him/her what you have written and what the Holy Spirit is speaking to you. You were never meant to go through this alone.

Conclusion

We've covered some heavy topics together, especially in the last chapter. But let's not forget this is a book about joy.

We live in a world where happiness and joy are talked about almost synonymously. There's a lot of overlap to be sure; but happiness depends on what's happening in our life, while joy is a byproduct of our deepest and most intimate relationships.

$C + P = E$ (our circumstances plus our perspective equals our experience). We have little or no control over much of our circumstances, but we have 100 percent control of our perspective.

This book could be little more than some great thoughts, inspiration, and a little help for the next few weeks in your journey toward a more joyful life. Or, this book could be the springboard to learning how to become joyful 90 percent of the time. Becoming a joyful person will take practice, and you will need to learn to practice asking yourself four strategic questions on a regular basis if you genuinely want to see long-term results:

1. Where's my focus?
2. What is my purpose?
3. Where is my hope?
4. What are my expectations?

I shared in the beginning of this book that after being a very optimistic, joyful, and upbeat person, I experienced a season of extended physical pain and emotional discouragement in which I lost my joy. It was subtle, but little by little I began to develop a mindset of negativity. I began to see the glass as "half full" in every situation and relationship. As the pain and circumstances continued to be challenging, I forgot all the good that God had done in my life. I was focused on what was lacking, asking God the question "Why me?" Instead, I should have been trusting Him and asking "What do You want me to learn, and how can You use this difficulty for Your glory?"

> I forgot all the good that God had done in my life. I was focused on what was lacking, asking God the question "Why me?"

This book in large measure was God's antidote to my lack of joy in my season of discouragement; but becoming aware of the problem did not change it. I actually went into training and began asking these questions on a regular basis every day when my spirits begin to droop, and when the melancholy feelings begin to invade my soul.

As I asked each question, I would snap out of my gloom and recognize my focus had shifted off of the Lord and others and onto myself. At other times, I would ask question number two, "What's my purpose?" I would realize God has bigger purposes for the challenges that I'm facing and He's working it out even when my circumstances remain the same.

I wrote these questions on a card. I kept them before me and practiced them when I began to lose perspective. Much like playing the piano, going to the gym, or learning to play a new sport, practice allowed the Spirit of God along with the truth of the Word of God to begin to renew my mind in such a way that new pathways were forming in my brain. As that happened, my perspective began to change on a regular basis. Perfect, no! Joyful on a regular basis, yes!

So, as we close our time together, I invite you to continue the journey. If you do, I can guarantee because of Jesus' love for you and His promises, your joy will return. In fact, joy is a fruit of the Spirit. As you continue to draw near to Jesus and renew your mind with His Word, His Spirit will manifest His peace and joy in your everyday experience.

There's no magic pill, and there's no quick fix. It is God who is at work in us, both to will and to work for His good pleasure. He gives us the truth and creates His desires within us *and* we have to make the effort; that's how grace works.

> There's no magic pill, and there's no quick fix. It is God who is at work in us both to will and to work for His good pleasure.

We can't change ourselves, but God never changes us without our cooperation—that's the "working out of our salvation/deliverance" that Paul will teach us in Philippians 2:12–13.

Few things are more contagious than meeting someone who has a genuinely joyful spirit, regardless of their circumstances. I can think of some very special people right now who make me smile whenever they come to my mind.

Life is hard, but God is good! Joy indeed is "the serious business of Heaven," as C. S. Lewis observed.

My prayer is that, if your life is going well, you might find an even deeper joy, rooted in an ever-growing intimacy with Jesus.

And if your life is not going well, that you might discover the transforming truth that joy is not something coming someday, some way, when everything gets better. Joy is a choice!

As for me, I've learned a lesson I pray I will never forget: *I choose joy!*

Acknowledgments

First and foremost, I want to acknowledge the patience and kindness of Jesus. Even after almost fifty years of walking together, I lost perspective and much of my joy. Thank *You*, Lord, for speaking to me and being so patient with me.

Second, to my wife, Theresa, I say thank you once again for your example, your kind and bold words that I needed to hear, and your amazing intercession for me and this book all along the way.

Third, a special thank you to Chris Tiegreen for his immensely invaluable work on the manuscript, and to Suzan Packee for the hours of carefully inserting multiple rounds of edits with multiple good suggestions.

Finally, thank you to the Moody Publishers team for embracing this project, with special thanks to Drew Dyck and Cheryl Molin.

Notes

1. C. S. Lewis, *Letters to Malcolm: Chiefly on Prayer* (Harvest, 1964), 93.
2. This is a paraphrase of Job 1:21.
3. Kevin McIntire, *Don't Google It: Cancer, Joy and Suffering: Not Necessarily in that Order* (pub. by author, 2020), 76.
4. Collins Online Dictionary, "vantage," https://www.collinsdictionary.com/us/dictionary/english/vantage.
5. Francis A. Schaeffer, *True Spirituality, in The Complete Works of Francis A. Schaeffer: A Christian Worldview,* vol. 3, *A Christian View of Spirituality* (Crossway, 1982), 345.
6. Rodney Stark, *The Rise of Christianity: A Sociologist Reconsiders History* (Princeton University Press, 1996), 5–6, 10, 74–83.
7. "God whispers to us in our pleasures, speaks in our conscience, but shouts in our pain: it is His megaphone to rouse a deaf world." C. S. Lewis, *The Problem of Pain* (HarperOne, 2001), 91.
8. Joni Eareckson Tada and Steve Estes, *When God Weeps: Why Our Sufferings Matter to the Almighty* (Zondervan, 1997), 84.

Also Available
THE CHIP INGRAM APP

Life-Changing Truth to Help You Grow Closer to God

Available at:

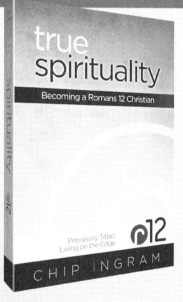

BIBLE STUDIES by
CHIP INGRAM

Available at **LivingOnTheEdge.org**